GREAT MYSTERIES

The Beginning of Language

OPPOSING VIEWPOINTS®

Look for these and other exciting *Great Mysteries: Opposing Viewpoints* books:

GREAT MYSTERIES

The Beginning of Language

OPPOSING VIEWPOINTS®

by Clarice Swisher

Greenhaven Press, Inc.   P.O. Box 289009, San Diego, California 92128-9009

Library of Congress Cataloging-in-Publication Data

Swisher, Clarice, 1933-
   The beginning of language / by Clarice Swisher.
     p.   cm. — (Great mysteries : opposing viewpoints)
   Bibliography: p.
   Includes index.
   Summary: Discusses historical, philosophical, and scientific theories about the mysterious origins of human language.
   ISBN 0-89908-064-2
   1. Language and languages—Origin—Juvenile literature.
[1. Language and languages—Origin.] I. Title. II. Series: Great mysteries (San Diego, Calif.)
P116.S85 1989
401—dc20
                                       89-7940
                                          CIP
                                          AC

*To my daughter Karin
who encouraged me
to undertake the project
of writing this book*

Contents

Introduction

This book is written for the curious—those who want to explore the mysteries that are everywhere. To be human is to be constantly surrounded by wonderment. How do birds fly? Are ghosts real? Can animals and people communicate? Was King Arthur a real person or a myth? Why did Amelia Earhart disappear? Did history really happen the way we think it did? Where did the world come from? Where is it going?

Great Mysteries: Opposing Viewpoints books are intended to offer the reader an opportunity to explore some of the many mysteries that both trouble and intrigue us. For the span of each book, we want the reader to feel that he or she is a scientist investigating the extinction of the dinosaurs, an archaeologist searching for clues to the origin of the great Egyptian pyramids, a psychic detective testing the existence of ESP.

One thing all mysteries have in common is that there is no ready answer. Often there are *many* answers but none on which even the majority of authorities agrees. *Great Mysteries: Opposing Viewpoints* books introduce the intriguing views of the experts, allowing the reader to participate in their explorations, their theories, and their disagreements as they try to explain the mysteries of our world.

But most readers won't want to stop here. These *Great Mysteries: Opposing Viewpoints* aim to stimulate the reader's curiosity. Although truth is often impossible to discover, the search is fascinating. It is up to the reader to examine the evidence, to decide whether the answer is there—or to explore further.

"Penetrating so many secrets, we cease to believe in the unknowable. But there it sits nevertheless, calmly licking its chops."

H.L. Mencken, American essayist

One

The Mystery of Language

Imagine that you have made plans to attend your favorite cousin's birthday celebration with your family on Friday evening. After you made the plans, your best friend invited you to a party to be held on the same Friday evening. You want to go to both, but have decided to attend the party. You need to tell your family that you will not be going to the relatives' house. The explanation sounds simple. But imagine also that no one has a language, no words to use.

How would you communicate your wishes without a language? You would probably behave much like a person playing charades, a game in which one person acts out a title and others guess what it is. Or you might act something like your dog when it wants a treat, barking, jumping, perking up its ears. Can you imagine using your arms, hands, and simple voice sounds instead of words? Using gestures and wordless sounds may get your point across, but not very efficiently. Talking with words, like many human abilities, is something most people take for granted, but people have not always had words to use.

Human beings perform many complex tasks without thinking about doing them. Unaware of their efforts, they walk and swallow and breathe and hear and speak. These are physical functions which both humans and animals do by instinct, but only humans can speak words. Talking in words is different from

This husband uses a combination of hand gestures
and words to convey a story to his wife.

Herodotus was a Greek historian who lived during the fifth century B.C.

the other functions because it must be learned from the environment. A baby's body will automatically swallow and breathe, but a baby will not automatically speak Chinese or Spanish unless it grows up in a Chinese- or Spanish-speaking environment. Humans have a special ability that allows them to learn words and compose sentences in the particular language of their upbringing.

How Did Language Begin?

Learning to speak a language is amazing enough when there are speakers to learn it from, but to originate a language is even more amazing. At an unknown time in an unknown place, someone spoke the first word. No one recorded the event; no one told about it. No one knows definitely when or where it happened or how or why it happened. For thousands of years, people have wondered and speculated about the origin of language, but it is still a mystery.

It seems to be part of human nature to want to solve mysteries. Because no records tell how language began, many people have developed theories. They have developed these theories in many different ways.

For example, Herodotus, an ancient Greek historian, told the story of an Egyptian interested in the origin of language. The Egyptian tried an experiment. He isolated two infants, keeping them entirely away from human voices. When they talked, he thought they would speak in the original language. Because one of the children said *bekos*, a word meaning "bread" in Phrygia, a Middle Eastern country, the Egyptian was sure that Phrygian was the original language. The story contains no information about the other child and what, if anything, it said.

Interested theorists have tried to answer one or more of these questions: Who first spoke? Where were the first words spoken? Why did people start using words? How could they make the sounds and give them meaning? What did the first words sound like?

This is a portion of a wooden Egyptian sarcophagus which shows the writing system used at the time. It probably tells, in part, the story of the life of the person buried in it.

When were the first words spoken? Journalists who write front-page news stories answer the who, what, when, where, why, and how questions in the opening paragraphs of their stories. They get the facts by covering an event in person, by getting information first-hand. Language theorists are handicapped. They try to answer their questions about an event that occurred at some prehistoric time—a very difficult task indeed. Investigating theories about language origin shows how complex language is and how difficult it is to find information. The mystery has no easy solution.

Language is very much a part of who each person is. It expresses ideas and feelings and influences success and happiness. For example, a student able to explain clearly to her parents why she wants to go on a field trip is more likely to be heard than another student who merely says, "Everybody's going."

Differences in expression make language personal and individual. At the same time, language belongs to the culture of a whole people. The Fijian language, for example, belongs to all Fijians and enables them to communicate with each other. Language works by rules, agreed upon by the majority of a group's speakers. Because of its dual nature—belonging both to the individual and to the group—solutions to language mysteries involve study of individual speakers

"A language is a communications system that is capable of transmitting new information."

Philip Lieberman, *On the Origins of Language*

"Although we now regard the communication of thought as the main object of speaking, there is no reason for thinking that this has always been the case; it is perfectly possible that speech has developed from something which had no other purpose than that of exercising the muscles of the mouth and throat."

Otto Jespersen, *Language: Its Nature, Development and Origin*

as well as group communication. Another reason the study of language is complex is that there is not one simple definition for the word *language*. Scholars differ when they use the word because language has several features.

What Is Language?

Some scholars focus on language as communication. Its main function is to let people give and receive messages. It is a partnership, they say, between speaker and listener, used to bring about mutual understanding. These scholars deny that language exists when a speaker merely cries out; voice sounds became words when one person intended his sounds to be heard and answered by another. For example, if a prehistoric woman saw a snake and cried *"ahhhh!"* to no one in particular, there would be no language. If she said *"ahhhh"* as a warning to her son, and he said *"ah-huh"* when he saw the snake, there would be communication and, thus, language.

An adult from the Tasaday tribe comforts and warns a child to watch out for sharp things.

Greek philosopher Aristotle uses language as a tool to teach Alexander the Great.

Other scholars focus on the mind of the speaker and the meaning behind the words. To these scholars, "language" is a term reserved for sounds humans make to express a *thought* originating in the brain. Language lets people think, and thinking gives them freedom and opportunity that animals do not have. For example, a young person can say, "Tomorrow I will mow the grass before I go to skating practice. Is that ok?" Thinking ahead offers the freedom to plan and the opportunity to gain approval. Animals, by contrast, make sounds by instinct, sounds they inherit and make automatically, just as they breathe or swallow. A dog barks at the mail carrier automatically in the same bark every day; it is not able to plan, "Today I won't bark."

Thinking in language, however, puts restrictions on freedom because groups agree to think in certain ways. For example, when the young person says, "Tomorrow I will mow the grass," the group expects the grass to be mowed. If it is, the group thinks the speaker is "responsible." If not, the group thinks the person is "careless." The language of the group thus influences and molds the mind of the individual.

Aristotle, an ancient Greek philosopher, said that language is "sound with a soul," with mind and personality. A modern scholar, James H. Stam, agreed

This macaw chatters to its mates in nearby trees.

with Aristotle. He said, "Parrots, musical instruments, even echoing rocks make sounds; but since . . . no . . . thought lies behind these sounds, we cannot conclude there is a soul either." In other words, language and thinking are tightly interwoven and originate together.

A third way to define language is to focus on its usefulness. Several scholars refer to language as a tool people use for their own purposes. They use it to get what they want, to get help, to pass on information, to express feelings. For example, it is more efficient to use the tool of language to say "I want a peach" than it is to take another by the hand, go to the refrigerator, and point to the peach and to the mouth— just as it is easier to use a shovel as a tool to dig a hole instead of pushing dirt away by hand.

Linguists tell us that an individual, as well as a society, has all the words it needs and no more. To illustrate, an Eskimo has many words for a seal: words for old ones and young, for seals in water or out. An American seldom needs more than *seal*, *sea lion*, and *pup*. The same is true for snow. An Eskimo has more than fifty words to name, for example, snow that is wet, dry, frozen, soft, falling, or fallen. English speakers get by with a half dozen words because snow is less crucial in their lives. Old English speakers had a total vocabulary of approximately fifty thousand words; modern English speakers have more than six hundred thousand tools, or words, to choose from. Since the very first speakers in prehistoric times had far fewer activities than we do, few belongings, and limited travel, their total vocabulary was probably very small.

Only Humans Have Language

A fourth view is that language sets humans apart from all other creatures. Some scholars ponder what makes human beings "human." They say that language, more than anything else, makes people human because they alone have it. Descartes, a seventeenth-century French philosopher, thought that speech set humans above both beasts and machines. Parrots can mimic words, dogs can respond to them, but only humans can invent them. These scholars say that language was invented when the human mind could invent words.

Finally, some scholars view the key to language as *creativity*. They place language in the same category as music and painting because words stimulate the imagination as do music and painting. They point out that words and the imagination create what does not even exist. For example, words and the imagination created Zeus and the thunderbolt, Sinbad the Sailor, and Cinderella. Haymann Steinthal, a nineteenth-century German philosopher, said that language is not a "thing like gunpowder," but "an event like an explosion." In other words, the importance of language

René Descartes reasoned that only humans are capable of language.

Words act as a creative force much as studying great works of art can stimulate the imagination.

is not the words and sentences themselves, but rather the creative outcome that results when the imagination has words to use for creating. An Arab proverb, echoing this view, says, "Language is the steed that carries one into a far country." Scholars who see language and creativity intertwined, as are language and thought, associate the origin of language with the first verbal creative expressions.

These five features show how complex language is; the variety underscores what a huge task it is to solve the mystery of its origin. Because language is many-sided, scholars disagree. For centuries they debated which theory was best, but they usually did not think their opponents were totally wrong. Recognizing the complexity of language, scholars eventually realized that no one could solve the mystery alone; they needed the ideas and research of other scholars.

How Is Language Origin Studied?

Over the years scholars from many fields have contributed theories and information. Until the mid-1800s, theologians, historians, and philosophers contributed most of the theories about language origin. Theologians, those who study religions, searched religious texts for clues. Many studied the Bible, the Judeo-Christian religious book. Historians used their knowledge of the past to develop origin theories. Philosophers used reason, or logical thinking, to conclude how language could most logically have originated.

During the eighteenth and nineteenth centuries, these scholars refined their theories by debating with one another at centers for scholarly study in Berlin and Paris. These centers were called *societies* or *academies*. In 1865 one of the centers, the Society of Linguistics in Paris, prohibited all studies of language origin because the question was "deemed unanswerable in a verifiable way." In other words, theologians', historians', and philosophers' theories could never be proved, or verified, because facts and evidence were unavailable. No records existed. The Paris Society took the position that speculation without fact was unworthy of debate. It appeared at the time that the mystery of the origin of language would remain unsolved.

Even though the Paris Society closed debate on the subject, the search went on. During the second half of the nineteenth century, many scholars began to use the methods of science. They found evidence, studied it, and drew conclusions. Many social and physical scientists gathered information for their own studies; later their data helped language theorists develop new theories that were, at least in part, verifiable.

A group of philosophers and linguists debate theories at the home of Denis Diderot, an eighteenth-century French scholar.

Today, most scholars work on small parts of big questions. For example, one scholar may study the voice mechanism, another search old texts. Language scholars hope that one day enough answers to small questions will be available to solve the big mystery.

Small Pieces of a Big Puzzle

Many different kinds of scholars have provided helpful information. *Psychologists* observe the behavior of babies and children. They want to discover how children learn and think. Further, they listen to babies' sounds and children's words, hoping to discover the order in which children learn sounds, words, and sentences. They want to know which comes first, *b* sound or *f* sound, naming words or action words, command sentences or descriptive sentences. The way modern children learn language may help solve the mystery of the way the first speakers learned.

Two psychologists work with a young child examining pictures of familiar objects to see if the child can name them.

By comparing and studying the skulls of a gorilla (left), Homo erectus (center), and a modern Chinese man (right), scientists are able to form theories about how the brain and language developed.

Psychologists and *biologists* study non-human primates, that is, apes, which include chimpanzees, gorillas, and orangutans. They study their social organization and communication. They study their brains and skulls and voice mechanisms. They compare their findings with the data physicians and neurologists gather on human brains, skulls, and voice mechanisms. Psychologists conduct experiments trying to teach primates to perform tasks and communicate. After four years of training, one chimp, Viki, learned to listen in on a party line telephone, and although she never said "hello" she did learn to say "mama," "papa," "cup," and "up." Other chimps are said to have learned to communicate in human language through gestures but not spoken words. Biologists' findings about today's primates may offer clues about the earliest primates and the humans who followed them on the evolutionary trail.

Paleontologists and *archaeologists* dig up and study fossils. They measure skull size for clues about the brain. Perhaps comparison of prehistoric skulls with modern chimpanzee, human baby, and human adult skulls will tell when the brain was developed enough for language. Archaeologists sift through old ruins for clues about social and cultural development. These clues may also help determine when early

Researcher Jill Millen holds up a set of keys
while the chimpanzee Leah signs "key."

These archeologists must dig and sift through layers of earth looking for fossils and artifacts to learn more about our ancestors.

humans needed words for their daily living. Scholars think that prehistoric people who moved and tooled huge rocks must have needed language to accomplish the job.

Anthropologists study today's primitive cultures. They study the social life, work, gestures, tools, and language of people who live today much as our prehistoric ancestors lived. Perhaps these primitive people of our time offer clues about the first speakers. Studying their vocabulary words for *breaking* and *pounding*, for example, may provide clues about the first vocabularies.

Linguists and *philologists* search old written texts and compare today's languages throughout the world. They look for patterns and trends in sounds, word forms, and grammar. They want to know what sounds and words appear in every language. Such patterns may offer clues that can be traced back to early languages that no longer exist.

All of these scholars contribute ideas and evidence to the larger mystery.

"The attempt at describing types of speech spoken in bygone ages, some of them as much as half a million years back, may well be derided as a piece of folly."

Leopold Stein, *The Infancy of Speech and the Speech of Infancy*

"The lack of direct data, while it is a formidable obstacle, is not necessarily an insuperable one, provided sufficient indirect data are available."

Grace de Laguna, *Speech: Its Function and Development*

The theories of philosophers and the evidence of scientists gradually came together when scholars began developing theories that integrated the two kinds of information. But they, too, encountered problems because the time being studied is long and the facts are few. Every stage backward in human development covers a larger number of years than the previous stage and contains fewer facts. J.G. Herder summed up the problems when he said that "the inquirer into origins treads an unsure path, because his is a path into obscurity."

Though the facts about those first speakers at the beginning of the path are few, we can imagine these people. Imagine women and children of long ago walking through long grasses and among trees searching for berries and herbs. Imagine men carrying sharpened sticks, working to kill an animal. Imagine all of them later, together around a campfire, working

Is this what family life may have looked like a million years ago? The adults are making and using tools made of bone and horn.

on tools, cooking, playing, eating, sleeping. Such activities, in the warm glow of the campfire, must have urged them to communicate with one another.

Scenes like the one described above are simple enough to visualize. Modern people speaking an advanced language can easily create dialogues appropriate for primitive people gathered around a fire. But people of long ago were forging a way to talk to each other for the first time. How did it happen?

Let us explore how the early students of language began the search for answers.

The Tasaday tribe are a small group of primitive people who live in a tropical rain forest on a rugged island in the Philippines. Perhaps anthropologists could learn something about the origins of language by studying these people.

Two

Where Does Language Come From?

As early students of language began searching for answers about the way language originated, they realized how complicated language is. Some of them thought it was so complex that humans could never have invented it by themselves. They thought language came to humans from some wise external source, and they developed theories about what the external source was.

Two features about language, discussed briefly in chapter 1, particularly puzzled philosophers. The first feature is that speakers learn language from the environment. As mentioned earlier, a Chinese-speaking person learns Chinese from Chinese-speaking people. Babies do not know any words, but they have parents and adults to teach them. The dilemma is this: Who taught the first speakers? Many people believe there was an original set of parents. They taught their children, and their children taught the next generation and on and on. That idea explains how language developed and spread, but it does not solve the mystery of the first speakers and *their* teachers. The problem, then, is to discover how the first speakers could have learned language without any human, speaking teachers.

This toddler is learning from his mother
through words as well as gestures.

The second feature, also discussed briefly in chapter 1, is that language is tightly intertwined with thinking. Thinking can invent language, and language makes thinking possible. The dilemma is this: How did early humans acquire one or the other, thinking or speaking, when they had neither? The mystery, then, is to discover how the language-thought process began.

In this sixteenth-century Bible illustration, God surveys his creation, from the lowliest creatures to Adam and Eve in the garden of Eden.

Philosophers thought and discussed. How could early humans start something that was too hard for them to start by themselves? Who could have taught them? Many drew their answers from Western culture's well-known creation story. The story says that God created the world and its inhabitants in six days. The first humans, named Adam and Eve, lived in a garden paradise, called Eden, with all other living creatures. When God created the world, all living creatures were established in an order, from lowest to highest, as if each were a link in a long chain. Each species—the tiger, the ant, the hawk, the pike, the ape—is a link, and human beings are the topmost link. God put them there. None changed places, and each species is different from every other species. This world order is called the Great Chain of Being. For six thousand years the world has been like this, the story says.

Search for a Teacher

Not all of the philosophers found the same answers when they read the creation story. Some used only a small part of it, others used more. Three theories developed, and all three explained how the early humans could get language without creating it themselves. First, some philosophers thought God was the source of language and thought. Their theory is called the *divine origin theory* . Second, others thought a special spirit dwelt within humans and was the source of language. Their theory is called the *inner spirit theory*. A third group of philosophers thought nature contained all knowledge and provided the source for language. Their theory is called the *nature theory*. Though these three theories have one point in common, an outside source, they otherwise do not agree.

For more than a century, philosophers and scholars debated about a source, or "teacher," that could have given humans a language. Some wrote essays that

"God, that all-powerful Creator of nature and architect of the world, has impressed man with no character so proper to distinguish him from other animals, as by the faculty of speech."

Quintilian, a first-century Roman rhetorician

"Language,—human language,—after all, is but little better than the croak and cackle of fowls, and other utterances of brute nature,—sometimes not so adequate."

Nathaniel Hawthorne, American author

28

drew responses from other scholars. Others offered lectures at the Paris or Berlin centers for study, often followed by responding lectures from others. Gradually the theories emerged. The scholars mentioned in this chapter were part of the long debate.

God the Teacher?

The Bible provided the starting point for the divine origin theory. Having searched the Bible for clues about origin, theologians cited passages from both Old and New Testaments. The Book of John, chapter one, in the New Testament says, ''In the beginning was the Word; and the Word was with God; and the Word was God.'' This passage was read as evidence that God has knowledge of language (the Word) and was the originator and the authority on the subject. Another passage came from Genesis, chapter three;

The divine origin theory says that Adam originally named all living creatures according to God's instructions.

it says, "And then He [God] brought all the animals to Adam to be named; and whatever the man called every living creature, that was its name. The man gave names to all the cattle, and to every bird of the air, and to every beast of the field." This passage was read as evidence that there was one original set of parents, whom God instructed, and their first words were names. From these passages and from the Great Chain of Being idea, philosophers developed the divine origin theory.

Frenchman Condillac believed that language was given to Adam and Eve by God.

The Divine Origin Theory

The theory of divine origin states that God had knowledge of language, and human beings received it by some mysterious process. In 1746, philosopher E.B. Condillac wrote in an "Essay on the Origin of Human Knowledge" that all mental activity and speech were "bestowed" upon "our first parents [Adam and Eve] . . . by extra-ordinary assistance from the Deity." Condillac meant that God gave both thinking and language to his human creatures by some "extra" or unusual "assistance." On the other hand, Gottfried Ploucquet, a German professor of philosophy and logic during the 1700s, said that God "directly instructed Adam." He thought God had created the whole order of language and had created Adam with the ability to learn it. To insure that Adam actually learned, God directly gave Adam lessons, Ploucquet thought. Gotthold Lessing, another German philosopher, argued for a third way humans could have received God's gift. By "miracle," he said, humans were instructed through conversation with "higher beings." In addition, God himself had come down to "converse with man." All three philosophers agreed that language came from God, but they differed about the process by which humans received it.

Gotthold Lessing thought that God had miraculously transferred the power of language to humans.

Other philosophers explained why they thought the divine origin theory was true. Johann Peter Süssmilch, in lectures he gave in 1756, argued that

The divine origin of language had a powerful and famous advocate in Goethe (left). Adam Smith (right) agreed, and argued that names were the first words.

the beauty and orderliness in language demonstrate that people could not have invented language by themselves. He went on to argue that all other theories about how humans could have received language were wrong; "divine origin was the only solution left," he said. Other philosophers argued that if God had created walking ability in human beings, then God also created language ability in them. Another German philosopher, Johann Wolfgang von Goethe, said, "If man was of divine origin, language was too."

Language Origin and the Bible

The theory that God first instructed Adam has further implications. Its supporters say it implies that the instruction was a single event that occurred at a particular place and time and that God taught Adam particular words. Proponents of the divine origin theory combined clues from the Bible with their own interpretations. First, they said the event took place in the Garden of Eden about six thousand years ago. The time was the golden age at the beginning of creation when Adam and Eve, the angels, and God communicated freely with one another.

Second, some theorists said that God taught Adam only names. Later, Adam and his descendants developed a complete language. Genesis says that God brought the animals to Adam to be named. A British philosopher, Adam Smith, agreed with this idea. He said in 1761 that language "began with giving proper names to particular and familiar objects." Things close at hand, he said, received individual names first, like *Rover* for a dog, *Sam* for a monkey. After that, Smith thought words developed in this order: common nouns (*dog*), adjectives (*tall*), prepositions (*over*), verbs (*crush*), pronouns (*she*), adverbs (*slowly*), and conjunctions (*but*). Smith thought that only single words existed at the beginning. Later, humans put the words together into sentences. Johann Georg Hamann, an eighteenth-century German philosopher who lectured at the Berlin Academy, thought God "molded" forms of expression to suit human understanding. God, he said, created language with the kinds of phrases and expressions the human mind, the topmost link, could most easily learn.

Johann Hamann taught that God created a language that only the human mind could learn.

Was Hebrew the first language? This modern man transcribes the ancient texts of the Torah.

Third, divine origin theorists said that God taught Adam in one language and later brought about the development of many languages. Most of the philosophers thought that Hebrew was the first language because Hebrew texts are some of the oldest written records. They thought Hebrew was the only language until the time of the tower of Babel. The story about building that tower appears in the Old Testament Book of Genesis. It seems that there were people who had great pride and thought they could be as great as God. They said, ''Come let us build ourselves a city, and a tower with its top in the heavens, and let us make a name for ourselves.'' If they could build a tower high enough, they thought, they would reach God's level. God thought these people had too much pride. To stop them, God caused all the workers to speak different languages and, because the workers were no longer able to communicate, the tower building failed. God ''scattered [the people] abroad from there over the

Did God create numerous languages to stop the builders of the Tower of Babel?

face of all the earth.'' When the workers settled in new places, the new settlements developed new languages, and Hebrew was no longer the only language.

Not everyone agreed that God taught Adam in Hebrew. A Swedish philologist thought that God spoke in Swedish, Adam in Danish, and the serpent in French. He made no mention of Eve's language. This amusing story illustrates the pride philosophers and linguists took in their own language, thinking theirs was the original language. As late as 1934 at a Turkish linguistics conference, one speaker argued that Turkish was the root of all languages. All words, he said, derive from *günes*, the Turkish word for *sun*.

Divine Origin Theory Discredited

Some philosophers disagreed with the very basis of the theory. A twentieth-century Dutch psychologist, Geza Révész, said that the whole idea of ''a first man'' and ''a first language'' begun six thousand years ago is a fantasy. One proof is that archaeologists have data showing that humans have existed on earth much longer than six thousand years.

Others, too, disagreed with one or more parts of the divine origin theory. Northrop Frye, an American linguist and literary critic, said that speech is not a gift; it has to be learned and worked at. In other words, language develops slowly, word by word, with effort on the part of the learner. Diedrich Tiedemann, a German philosopher, argued that if God had created language, it would be perfect, but it is not and never was. J.G. Herder argued that if God had created language, it would not change, but it does. American sociologist A.S. Diamond said ''What would possess this speechless anthropoid to begin his career as a man by giving names to the animal kingdom, or a few objects around him?'' Diamond thought that early people spoke first because they needed help with their work and that they first used verbs (action words) instead of nouns (naming words).

''Language arose from the need and purpose of communication between man; and above all it arose from the communication of requests for assistance.''

A.S. Diamond, *The History and Origin of Language*

''It is claimed that men invented speech in order to express their needs; that seems to me an untenable opinion.''

Jean-Jacques Rousseau, *Essay on the Origin of Languages*

By the mid-nineteenth century, most scholars had rejected the divine origin theory of language. Even though this theory provided one solution to the mystery of the first "teacher" and the mystery of a source for thinking and speaking, philosophers thought there were better explanations. They had rejected a divine source, but they had not rejected the idea that language originated outside of the human mind. If God was not the source of language, what was?

Is a Mysterious Inner Spirit the Source of Language?

Out of the extensive debate that went on throughout the 1700s and beyond, other philosophers developed the inner spirit theory. The theory is based on the idea that a spirit resides within human beings, but this spirit is not a part of the human mind. This spirit, philosophers said, is the source of the first words. Once humans had the first words, they could continue to develop language because they were created with a special ability for language.

The philosophers described the inner spirit in different ways. They made it sound like a mysterious power. Wilhelm von Humboldt, a German philosopher from the early 1800s, saw language as "something directly given" and governed from the inside by "inner linguistic sense." Out of that sense, "man spins

Wilhelm von Humboldt believed language developed from an internal human sense.

language out of himself'' by a process of "fate.'' He said that the spirit is a "sense'' that is destined to provide knowledge and language. In an essay, "On the Origin of Language,'' nineteenth-century philosopher Friedrich Nietzsche said the inner spirit is "instinct,'' the innermost "kernel'' of one's being. According to Nietzsche, the inner spirit or instinct is inherited, unconscious knowledge.

August Schleicher, a German who studied theology, philosophy, and philology, thought that the inner spirit's main task was to form language. He described the spirit as living within the body, forming words and phrases, and giving them to the mind. Johann Jakob Bachofen, another German philosopher, referred to the inner spirit as a "symbol . . . in the most hidden depth of the soul.'' As a "symbol'' the inner spirit represents the power of knowledge hidden in some mysterious way within a person's soul, yet it is not part of the mind.

When they identified the inner spirit, all of these philosophers used words that suggest mystery: a "sense,'' a "kernel,'' a "symbol.'' That mysterious power gave language to the first speakers; what those speakers said was the origin of language.

The theory goes on to explain how the inner spirit worked and what sounds were first spoken. In this

Both Nietzsche (left) and Johann Bachofen (right) agreed that the power of language comes from an inner spirit. Nietzsche called it instinct and Bachofen called it the soul.

part of the explanation, the inner spirit sounds less like a mysterious power and more like a physical reaction.

According to this theory, language originated in two stages. In the first stage, the inner spirit made outcries from feelings or emotions. Haymann Steinthal, a linguistics professor from Berlin, thought the soul was forced to "break out in sounds," sounds that resulted from the emotions of pleasure or pain. The sounds were the same kinds that modern people make. Modern people say "*aaaah*" or "*ooooh*" in reaction to sudden delight; they say "*ouoo*" or "*ufff*" when they stub their toes hard. At this early stage, however, the sounds had no meaning and could not be repeated by intention. In other words, an early speaker, stubbing a toe two days later, could not intentionally say "*ouoo*." Some other natural cry might be made instead, until the time when *ouoo* became the word for hurt.

The second stage in the theory accounts for meaning. Because humans were the topmost link in

These university track team members respond to victory with shouts of joy.

Lobo, a Tasaday boy, speaks to a favorite bird
named Lemokan. The Tasaday believe certain birds
are messengers to and from the Owner of All Things.

the Great Chain of Being and had been created with special capacity for language, they gave sounds meaning. Over time a sound came to be associated with a particular experience, like *ouoo* with hurt. Eventually, that sound came to symbolize, or stand for, that experience in speakers' and listeners' minds. Whatever sound the inner spirit caused an early human to say upon finding good, sweet berries or hitting an elbow on a tree trunk became the words for those experiences, but only when the speakers and listeners in the group recognized that the sounds referred to the experiences.

Humans Are Predisposed to Language

This theory became known as the *whistle-and-grunt theory*, the *ee-ee theory*, the *ouch-ouch theory*, or the *pooh-pooh theory*. The names are sounds the inner spirit "burst forth" and made.

Philosophers who developed this theory had several reasons to believe it was true. First, the idea that an inner spirit resides within every object and living thing is an old idea, common in primitive cultures. People in primitive cultures often believe, for example, that every tree has a live, inner tree spirit, every camel a live, inner camel spirit, and every human a live, inner human spirit. Its presence means there is life within the object or creature. The idea is called *animism*. It made sense to philosophers that the powerful and mysterious human inner spirit knew language. Furthermore, philosophers could hear that humans and animals made sounds, sounds they did not intend to make and had not thought about first. If these sounds had not originated with thought, in the human brain, they must have had a different source within the body. Dogs bark, cattle low, horses neigh, birds sing, and humans cry out spontaneously without thought or intent. Both humans and animals vary their sounds for different experiences. Since humans were created with a special capacity for language, the theor-

This red-winged blackbird sings instinctively.

An Eastern timberwolf howls. Is her cry the same
as that of her ancestors, unchanged through time?

ists reasoned that humans were capable of hearing the variations in sound, repeating them, and giving them meaning to become words.

In short, the inner spirit theory explains the two dilemmas cited at the beginning of the chapter. By identifying the inner spirit as the source of language, it solves the first dilemma of "teacher." By determining that humans have a special capacity for language, the theory solves the second dilemma, the source of thought.

The inner spirit theory, like the divine origin theory, had its critics in the 1700s as well as later. A twentieth-century Dutch psychologist, Geza Révész, said that animal sounds used for communication are unlike true language sounds because they are instinctive and incapable of change or development. He went on to say that language, "even in its most primitive form, must have been a creation of the human mind."

By whistling through their hands, the Tasaday imitate Lemokan's song.
They interpret the bird's song and flight as warnings.

Leopold Stein attacked the inner spirit theory because of the way it was developed. He said that it should be ignored because it was derived from "speculation," not from facts. Others simply called the theory "unsatisfactory" and dismissed it as too vague and too mysterious, even though it supported the idea that humans were created with an ability to learn language.

Does Language Originate in Nature?

The same long-term search for a source or "teacher" that might have given language to humans produced a third theory that also said language originated outside the human mind. This was the nature theory based on an idea just as mysterious as the inner spirit idea. This theory said that language, its vocabulary and word order, is inherent in, or built into, nature and the orderly way God created it in the beginning. Language exists in nature in much the same way that gravity is a law of nature. The theorists thought that humans would automatically discover words and sentences in nature which contained God's knowledge and arrangement. Nature was not the "teacher"; it made knowledge of language available, and humans had a special ability to find it. Even though he disagreed with the theory, modern psychologist Geza Révész helps explain it. He says that nature's source of language was seen as a power above "human wisdom" that people obtain from nature without conscious effort. In other words, nature contains the knowledge of language and humans obtain it without intent and without effort.

Of the two stages described in this theory, the first is more important. It explains how humans got words from nature; the second explains how words acquired meaning.

Humans were able to obtain language from nature because they could imitate. Primitive people, out in nature all the time, heard its sounds. Then they used their voices to imitate the sounds they heard. Humans,

"Primitive language first appeared as an *invention*, introduced by some extraordinary member of the species."

Hilary Putnam, in
Language and Learning

"The origin of language is not so much invention as discovery, man's discovery of the world about him."

James H. Stam, *Inquiries into the Origin of Language*

equipped with a special capacity for language, imitated the sounds with no effort and found the wisdom or meaning. Imitating the sounds was the origin of language, according to this theory.

In the 1840s a German philosopher, Gotthelf Heinrich von Schubert, explained the process this way: He spoke of a "symphony of natural sounds" producing "music of the spheres." Language originated, he said, when humans "sang along with the melody of the stars and planets." Others describing the same theory spoke about humans imitating animals, rain, and thunder, sounds closer within earshot than the celestial spheres! For example, a primitive person might have said "*whoosh*" in response to wind, "*boom*" to thunder, "*pitter-patter*" to rain, "*honk*" to geese, and "*cuckoo*" to a songbird. Making the sounds of nature was the first important stage.

Responding to sounds of nature, such as thunder, may have been the way humans first spoke.

The second stage established the sounds as words. Over time and with repetition, the imitated sounds represented the actual sound. For example, *cuckoo* was at first an imitation of a bird's song. Eventually *cuckoo* became the word that *named* the sound and then named the bird. *Cuckoo* was no longer only a sound; it took on meaning. In modern language, words whose sounds imitate their meanings are called *onomatopoeic* words.

This theory became known as the *bow-wow theory* or the *ding-dong theory*. The names came from sounds the theorists imagined the first speakers to have made.

Philosophers who proposed the nature theory also had reasons to believe their theory to be true. They had thought about knowledge and wondered about what was true. Human minds, in their limited ways, know that some things are true, but humans are often wrong. There must be a source of truth that cannot be wrong, philosophers thought, and concluded that it is nature. Language, a part of nature's truth, is there for humans to discover, they said.

The idea of a transfer from nature's truth to human words is as old as Plato, a Greek philosopher from the fourth century B.C. He said there is a connection between the names of things and the things themselves, a bond that guided the naming of objects and experi-

Might a primitive person have watched geese like these, reproduced the "honk," and eventually used the word to mean the animal?

ences. In the 1860s, Max Müller, a German philosopher, explained the same idea this way: He said there is a correspondence, or connection, "between sound and sense, by a law of nature, a mysterious law of harmony." The word *harmony* is important because it suggests that the "correspondence" between the word and object has a right and pleasant way of fitting together. For example, *sun* is the right sound for the big hot ball of fire.

Johann Georg Hamann, the eighteenth-century German philosopher, explained how humans discovered nature's truth. He used comparisons. "Language is like fire," he said; it must be discovered the same way Newton discovered gravity. He said that language is like a continent; Columbus did not invent America, he discovered what was already there.

Sir Isaac Newton did not invent gravity; he discovered its presence, in the same way some people believe language was discovered.

The nature theory provides an answer to the first dilemma—the "teacher"—but answers the second—the source of thought—only by implication. By saying that nature contains the truth of language and humans can discover it by imitating it, the theory shows how humans acquired language without teachers. By implication, once humans had words, they could think and figure out the rest of language.

The nature theory, like the others, had its critics and opponents. Geza Révész thought the whole idea of knowledge in nature, or "wordless thought" existing before there were words, was a "senseless idea." Leopold Stein, author of *The Infancy of Speech and the Speech of Infancy*, thought it was a "dangerous" approach to be guided by "preconceived plans and patterns," referring to the idea that language truth had always existed in nature. The opponents to the nature theory said that human speakers *intend* to speak, they *vary* the language, and they *choose* words for their use. The nature theory denied these choices.

There were a few philosophers who thought that the nature theory needed a "teacher." They proposed the idea that poets were the teachers of nature's language. Poets, they thought, had greater skill for hearing the language of nature. They also had the skill to put it into words and stories. Ralph Waldo Emerson,

"Words and forms need not be sought, they would appear of their own accord."

W. Wundt, *Die Sprache*

"Language as such, even in its most primitive form, must have been a creation of the human mind."

G. Révész, *The Origins and Prehistory of Language*

The poet Emerson would agree with the sing-song theory because he believed that words come from nature.

"Men sang out their feelings long before they were able to speak their thoughts."

Otto Jespersen, *Language: Its Nature, Development and Origin*

"Man's capacity to sing is probably the slow product of his evolution since language appeared."

A.S. Diamond, *The History and Origin of Language*

a nineteenth-century American philosopher, said that the poet "puts eyes and a tongue into every dumb and inanimate object." He suggested that poets have keener vision to see objects and greater imagination to give them names. He said that all poetry was written "before time was." He meant that poets get their words from nature, and nature contains truth that has always existed.

Poets and Language

Philosophers suggested a number of ways that poets receive the language from nature and in turn "teach" it to others. John Brown, an English philosopher who wrote in 1763, thought the original language occurred as an "abrupt outburst" in poetry, song, and dance. Others thought the poets first chanted. Others thought nature's language came to poets in dreams or in picture language that they later formed into stories and myths. Since Hebrew and Greek are among the oldest known languages, some thought the original poets were Moses, who brought the Ten Commandments to the Hebrews, and Homer, the Greek poet who wrote the *Iliad* and the *Odyssey*. The theory that poets were the "teachers" of nature's language became known as the *sing-song theory*, named from the rhythm of poetry.

Johannes Schmidt thought that the bow-wow theory was ridiculous.

After 1900 few scholars believed the theories that either a divine or special power was the origin of language. The idea no longer fit the facts that scientists were discovering from fossils and from studies in linguistics. No longer was language seen as an outburst or an imitation. It was now seen as an expression a speaker *intended* to make, a message spoken to someone. The old ideas, Révész said, were ''wrong in principle,'' wrong in their idea. Johannes Schmidt criticized Christoph Voigtmann, who claimed words imitate nature's sounds, as ''the chief cuckoo.'' It was time for new theories about the origin of language.

Three

Did the Human Mind Create Language?

Were human beings given a language by a wise, mysterious power beyond themselves, or did they invent it with their own intelligence? These two questions imply that the mystery of language origin can be reduced to a simple either-or answer. While that idea may work well for organizing chapters in a book, the actual mystery is more complex. The word *origin* itself has more than one definition.

In the late 1760s, J.G. Herder, winner of the prize essay on language at the Berlin Academy, identified three pertinent definitions for *origin*. First, it means *causes*. Investigating the causes of language means searching for the reasons humans developed it. Did they need words for their work? for protection against danger? for pleasure and play? Did they develop language merely because their brains and voices were able to invent words with meanings? Causes are part of the mystery.

Second, *origin* means *source*. Investigating the source of language means asking over and over, "What came before?" If language scholars are able to identify the first words, they ask what came before the words. If they go back to gestures, they ask what came before those. They repeat the question until they can think of no more possibilities for "what came

These construction workers need language in order
to work together to accomplish their goal. Did our
ancestors develop language for the same purpose?

"Many animals make complex sounds, of course, but only in humans do those sounds represent objects or events in an arbitrary yet symbolic way."

Richard E. Leakey and Roger Lewin, *People of the Lake: Mankind and Its Beginnings*

"The speech of some animals may be more like our language than most people are willing to admit."

Otto Jespersen, *Language: Its Nature, Development and Origin*

before." Then, they think, they have arrived at the source. Solving the mystery of the source of language yields answers different from those explaining its causes.

Third, *origin* means *beginning*. Investigating the beginning focuses on when and how the first words were spoken and what the words were like. Scholars searching for the beginning need a clear definition of language. Are they searching for the first sound? word? sentence? conversation? Explaining the first sounds and how they were made is different from an explanation of the first conversation.

Causes, source, beginning—the three definitions lead scholars in different directions; their answers reflect different angles on the same mystery.

How Were the First Words Made?

The three theories in chapter 2 explained three searches for the source of language. God, the inner spirit, and nature were scholars' final answers to the question "What came before?" Theories to be discussed in chapter 3 answer scholars' questions about the beginning of language. The underlying question for all the theories is this: How did the first words come about and what were they like? In addition, the search for the beginning leads scholars to clarify the difference between humans and animals because the use of sentences composed of words made with phonetic sounds is distinctly human.

All of the theories discussed in both chapters 2 and 3 evolved out of the philosophical discussion about language origin carried on during the eighteenth and nineteenth centuries. Theories did not develop in neat sequential order, popping into line like soldiers in a row; rather one theory overlapped another, one theorist leaping ahead with a new idea, another going back to an old one.

Many eighteenth- and nineteenth-century philosophers were uncomfortable with the idea that early humans went dumbly about their daily business while language was being given to them. Or they were uncomfortable with the idea that humans discovered language without consciously knowing that they were discovering anything. They liked much better the idea that early humans took an active part, solved problems for their needs, produced what they intended to produce, and used their creative intelligence. Philosophers' theories discussed in this chapter focus on language beginnings and can loosely be classified as *invention theories*. How did humans invent language, they wanted to know. Let us look at the answers that six philosophers gave.

Three Invention Theories

A German philosopher, Friedrich von Schlegel, thought that early humans invented a full-blown language all at once. He used the analogy of a cave painting. A cave painting is an artist's whole conception drawn as a complete picture. It is not developed

These prehistoric paintings of reindeer, horses, and bulls were done on the walls of Lascaux cave in southwest France almost 17,000 years ago. The artists who created these animals were also hunters who needed a system of communication to live and work.

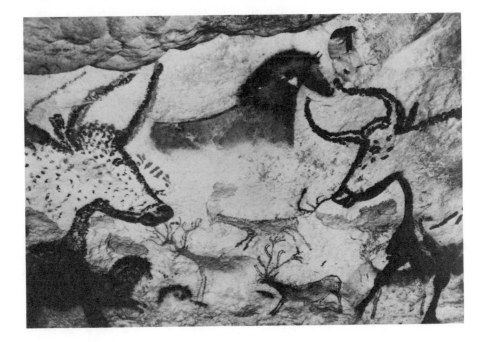

Friedrich von Schlegel (left) equated the origin of language with early cave paintings. Both, he said, began as complete units. Friedrich Engels (right) wrote that language was tied to work.

one line at a time over many years. Likewise, language developed as a completed unit, he thought.

Schlegel, who published his philosophy of language in 1830, was a member of a philosophical group interested in the source of language. He and others discussed the idea that a complete knowledge of language had mysteriously existed before God spoke and revealed it. Chapter 2 explains the theory that God created language and made it part of the knowledge of nature. Schlegel suggested that God mentally created the plan of language first; when nature was created, God articulated language, or "broke the silence." When the time came for humans to invent language, their methods to reveal their knowledge echoed God's original way of breaking the silence. In other words, humans, too, created language in their minds before speaking a word.

Schlegel did not mean that the first speaking humans had a rich vocabulary and perfect grammar. He did mean that "the first formations of the earliest languages were not possible until the essential idea of language . . . had taken root in the human consciousness." By the "essential idea," he meant 1) that the speaker intended mutual communication with another speaker; that is, one person spoke directly to another who understood the message, 2) that the speaker used words with phonetic sounds; that is, he used vowels and consonants, not natural cries of pain or pleasure, and 3) that his words were symbols; that is, his words represented objects and experiences not momentarily present. In other words, Schlegel thought the mind had to comprehend all three parts before language was possible. When all the parts were present, the speaker spoke a language as complete as an artist's whole reindeer carved on a cave wall. The techniques and details developed further, but the idea or concept was complete at the outset.

Friedrich Engels had a different idea; he thought language originated as early humans worked together. A German social scientist who was also interested in anthropology, Engels developed his ideas between 1872 and 1882. He was particularly interested in the difference between the way humans and animals relate to nature. He observed that animals live in nature and use it. In contrast, humans make nature serve them; they master it with their work. Engels thought "it is labour" that distinguishes humans from animals, not language, as many thought. Out of his observations about the way humans master nature, Engels developed his theory about the way humans invented language.

This beaver works with his natural surroundings to manufacture his home. But, farmers harness the land, planting and reaping their crops, making nature work for them.

Primitive people invented language as they worked together to get food and to make tools and houses. "In short, men in the making arrived at a point where *they had something to say* to one another," Engels wrote. For example, one may need to say to another "*run*" while hunting, "*pound*" while making a tool, or "*push*" while moving logs for a house. He went on to explain that talking developed speech organs; working and talking led to further brain development, and the brain further developed language. The first things "men in the making" had to say, Engels thought, sounded like rhythmic chants they invented while working together. This theory came to be known as the *yo-he-ho theory* because *yo-he-ho* has a rhythm to help workers time their efforts to push a rock into place.

These builders may have used a rhythmic chant to coordinate their movements while maneuvering the huge stones.

Jeremy Bentham, an English philosopher who lived from 1748 to 1832, developed a "supply and demand theory of words." As human needs demanded words, the human mind supplied them, "something like a primitive business proposition." Bentham thought of language as a tool that was invented, just as a pounding implement was. He thought early people invented language tools that supplied the demands of survival, enjoyment, and prevention of pain. At its earliest stage, speakers had no language for ideas or reflection.

Words as Sentences

The first words were invented, Bentham thought, for making commands and transactions to satisfy necessary wants and desires, like gathering food, scaring dangerous animals, building fires. He thought that "single primitive utterances"—or "words"—were equal to whole sentences. For example, the word *go* would equal the whole sentence, "Go to the creek and wash the blood off this knife." Language progressed when the speakers broke down "primitive one-word sentences into their component parts." Underlying Bentham's entire theory is the idea of

Jeremy Bentham's theory revolved around the human need for language as a tool.

These Tasaday men work together to build a fire, taking turns spinning the end of the stick against a flat piece of wood. The children are not permitted to make fire.

scarcity; primitive humans said only what was necessary and spoke only the minimum number of words.

Supply-and-demand language invention might have gone this way: A father saw his daughter about to hit her head on the cave ceiling. Because he wanted to prevent her pain, he invented the word *dop*. Later, out in the woods, he noticed a dangerous animal near his daughter. He used the word he invented, *dop*, to warn her of the danger nearby. As he used *dop* over and over to warn of danger or pain, it took on the meaning of the sentence, "Watch out!" With further development, it was broken down into more refined parts, "Watch out for the lion," or "Don't hit your head." In sum, according to Bentham's theory, the first speakers invented language in short form to use as tools to supply them with necessities for their simple lives.

Two Gesture Theories

Diedrich Tiedemann, who published *Attempt at a Clarification of the Origin of Language* in 1772, thought language began with gestures. He based his theory on the idea that "man was always a rational creature, and at all times could correctly judge how his need for mutual communication could be most appropriately satisfied." He meant that humans had always been able to figure out correctly what they needed and the best way to get what they wanted.

Tiedemann thought the process of language began this way: The first humans lived happily for a time in an animal state. Gradually, they wanted to form groups, and they needed a way to communicate. They came up with the idea of using signs or gestures. According to Tiedemann, that development marked the beginning of language. Soon, however, they saw that a system of gestures alone was inadequate. Then they noticed two new things: that they themselves made sounds to express emotions and that animals used sounds efficiently. They figured out, then, that they could use sounds, instead of gestures, as signs for their thoughts.

According to Tiedemann's theory, these early people could carry on mental conversations with themselves before they had words. One of them might think this sequence to himself: "These gestures aren't working very well. When that dog barks, the birds fly away. The dog's sounds are very effective. I make sounds when I get hurt. I think we humans should use our voice sounds as animals do; instead of hand signs, we could use our voices to communicate our thoughts." Tiedemann's theory never explained how that early person could think those thoughts before he had a language; Tiedemann said he assumed humans always could reason. Lazarus Geiger, a professor of philosophy, agreed with Tiedemann. He thought language must have been the "personal creation of one or more linguistically gifted individuals." Gifted people were better able to form thoughts before they were able to speak them, he thought.

Gesturing alone is not enough to get this woman's point across to the others in her group; she also uses persuasive words.

This little girl is intently trying to coordinate her hand movements while unconsciously opening her mouth.

Sir Richard Paget, an English scientist, developed the *ta-ta theory*, a theory that said language began with mouth gestures. The theory suggests that early speakers moved tongue, lips, and jaw, mimicking their hand actions. To compare, modern children move their jaws up and down as they learn to cut with scissors.

Early humans began communication silently, suggested Paget, using only their mouths and hands. Next, they added sounds as their mouths moved. They came to realize, first, that they needed their hands for other things and, second, that their mouths and sounds were all that were necessary to communicate. Both Paget's theory and Tiedemann's theory said that language began with gestures, and both assumed that humans could reason before they had words, an idea contrary to what most other language scholars believe. Paget's theory is called the *ta-ta theory* because those sounds easily accompany a mouth opening and closing in imitation of hand action.

In the late 1760s, J.G. Herder, a German philosopher, proposed that language began in silent reflection. Herder thought that the ability to reflect,

Before an audience of scientists, Sir Richard Paget demonstrates a machine he made which mimics a human voice.

to think, was by nature characteristic of all humans. According to Herder's theory, a series of observations and thoughts began in sensations and ended in naming. His theory was that language developed in several steps. First, a person confronted hundreds of sights, sounds, and other sensations from the environment. They flooded into the mind as unordered impressions. Second, some impressions were selected and given more attention. Third, a single object was concentrated on, its features noticed, and identified. Fourth, one feature was singled out that particularly marked the object. Fifth, the feature became the "words of the soul" or the "distinguishing words." And, thus, Herder said, language originated.

Herder offered this example of his reflective theory: A man saw a lamb and a multitude of sense impressions entered his mind—the lamb's color, its curly fleece, its wobbly legs, its odor. He reflected. He concentrated on the lamb and noticed its bleating sound. He reflected. Then he said to himself, "So! You are the bleating one!" According to Herder, the man's identification of the lamb as the "bleating one" was, in effect, naming the lamb, and he had invented language. At that point, by naming the feature— bleating—the man had invented language in his mind; he may never have said "So! You are the bleating

If this primitive man made a connection between the sound a lamb made and the animal itself, then he invented language.

Philosopher John Locke linked the formation of language to the development of reasoning.

one!'' out loud. For Herder, language began in the mind with reflection.

The six theories—Schlegel's full-blown language, Engels's yo-he-ho theory, Bentham's supply and demand theory, Tiedemann's gesture theory, Paget's ta-ta theory, and Herder's reflection theory—try to solve the mystery of how early people invented language at its start. All were concerned about the way words came to be. But instead of the invention of words, an English philosopher from the seventeenth century, John Locke, was interested in the invention of thought. He developed a theory explaining how he thought humans began the process of reasoning. His theory is similar to Herder's reflection theory.

The Invention of Thought

Locke developed a theory of simple, complex, and general ideas. *Tabula rasa* (a blank slate), he called it. The five senses (sight, sound, taste, smell, touch) send messages that are recorded in the blank mind. Locke called these sensations ''simple ideas.'' Then the mind associates one sensation with another and sees that some are alike and some are different. Locke called this mental activity ''reflection.'' Then the mind associates ''simple ideas'' to see how they are alike and different. With that process, the mind forms ''complex ideas.'' In the next step the mind sorts the ''complex ideas,'' separating some and connecting others. As a result, it forms ''general ideas.''

The process might go like this. A primitive woman tastes a green berry. Her taste buds send a ''sour'' sensation to her brain. She tastes many green berries. Her mind reflects that all green-berry sensations are ''sour.'' She has now formed a ''simple idea.'' Later, in the fall, the same woman tastes first one and then several purple berries and forms a second ''simple idea'' that purple berries are ''sweet.'' Next, she reflects that purple berries are unlike green berries, forming a ''complex idea.'' When, over time, she associates green berries with the summer season and purple berries with a later season, she forms a "general idea." That is, in summer berries are green and sour; in fall they are purple and sweet. In short, humans invent thought by reflecting about sense perceptions and then sorting them into categories by observing the similarities and differences. Locke coined the phrase "association of ideas" for this process.

The philosophers' theories discussed in this chapter identify humans as inventors of language and inventors of thought. As mentioned in chapter 1, philosophers agreed that thought and language are interdependent; it takes one to have the other. Together thought and language distinguish humans from animals. Though scholars disagree on many things, most do agree that the dual presence of speaking and thinking identifies humans as different from animals.

Humans, Animals, and Language

Why did humans invent thought and language while animals did not? J.G. Herder said that any theory of origin must distinguish that difference between humans and animals because the issue is also part of

A primitive woman tastes a green berry which is sour and eventually forms the simple idea that all green berries are sour.

"Language was complete at its beginning, the spontaneous creation of individuals and groups together."

Ernest Renan, *On the Origin of Language*

"It would seem that the acquisition of spoken language during human evolution should be viewed as a stepwise process."

Richard E. Leakey, *The Making of Mankind*

the mystery. Three scholars' explanations are presented here. Herder said humans had a nature different from animals; Darwin said humans are more capable than animals; and Müller said that intent and phonetic sounds set humans apart.

J.G. Herder's explanation of the difference between humans and animals goes back to the Great Chain of Being idea. Herder never mentioned that idea directly, but his explanation strongly suggests that he assumes humans are the topmost link. Herder said that according to "natural law," humans have a "nature" different from animals. Animals, he said, have keener instinct, keener inherited knowledge, to help them with food gathering, nest building, and protection. On the other hand, humans by their "nature" have a broader range of mental abilities. They can use their senses, their memory, and their reason as "modes of a single power." In other words, people have the ability to combine the different abilities and make them work together to form one, more powerful ability. For example, a human can see a woolly lamb and hear its bleating; at the same time she recalls similar lambs she has seen and heard before. She can reason that all lambs bleat. The three abilities—senses, memory, and reason—work together as one. As a result, people can select some out of many impressions, discard some and keep others, and see similarities and differences. Like Locke, Herder called this ability "reflection."

By referring to "human nature," he suggested that humans are and have always been equipped mentally with more abilities than animals have. Further, his explanation suggests, as in the Great Chain of Being idea, that humans are the topmost link.

A Difference in Degree

Charles Darwin, a scientist who wrote during the second half of the nineteenth century, said that the difference between humans and animals is a difference "in degree not in kind." Referring to all living creatures as "animals," Darwin said that "the lower animals differ from man solely in [man's] . . . larger power of associating sounds and ideas." For example, a human can better visualize an unseen lamb than an animal can. The person associates either the bleating sound or the word *lamb* with his or her memory of a lamb. Darwin suggested that animals can associate sounds and ideas, but humans have more ability, a "larger power," to make the connections between them.

Darwin also saw living creatures arranged in a continuous chain from simple animals to human beings, but he saw "no distinct break between them." He saw no gap between all the animals grouped together and humans grouped separately, as Herder did. Darwin said that the greater efficiency of the human brain led to more articulate speech, and speech, in turn, further developed the efficient human brain. He thought humans were especially endowed "with a capacity and inclination for language."

Both Herder and Darwin agreed that the world of living creatures is ordered from simplest to most complex. Both Herder and Darwin agreed that humans have greater mental ability and thus are capable of thought and language. Their point of disagreement lay in the placement of humans and the species just below them. Herder saw a definitive difference between animals and humans; Darwin saw more equal progression between all creatures, with only a degree of difference between people and other animals.

Humans Make Phonetic Sounds

Max Müller, a German philosopher who wrote during the mid-nineteenth century, identified two features of language that he said distinguished humans from animals: intent and phonetic sounds. Unlike animals, people can intentionally make a variety of sounds that have specific meanings.

Charles Darwin reasoned that since humans have greater mental capacity than animals, they are capable of thought and language.

This evolutionary chart was drawn in 1876 for a book written by Ernst Haeckel,
the first German advocate of Darwin's theories. It shows the process
of the development of life from a protoplasm to a Papuan man.

Müller acknowledged that animals communicate in a kind of language. He called the language common to both humans and animals "interjections," which he defined as expressive cries made in response to pleasure and pain. As cited earlier, interjections, or cries, are spontaneous sounds like *ahhh* and *ouoo* in humans, the bark of a dog, the meow of a cat. The ability to speak interjections is an inherited ability that both humans and animals know by instinct. Throughout the world all species of a kind make the same interjection sounds because they are born with the knowledge of those sounds. A collie that barks in Alaska sounds the same as a collie that barks in Poland. These interjections are responses; they are not made by intent. In other words, no act of will decides that an animal will make a cry of interjection. Müller suggested that when a stranger walks up to the door, no dog contemplates, "Shall I bark today or not? I guess I will." Animals are different because their language is not spoken by intention.

Max Müller pointed out the differences between human and animal communication.

This dog barks instinctively at the animal he has chased up a tree.

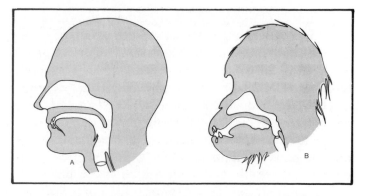

Sketches of the vocal tract mechanisms of an adult human (A) and an orangutan (B).

Not only can humans speak a language by intention, but they can also speak a different kind of sound. Humans can speak a phonetic language, but animals cannot. Humans can speak in vowels and consonants because they have a voice mechanism capable of making the sounds and a brain capable of combining them. For example, the voice can make *f-u-n* separately, and the brain can combine them into *fun*. Phonetic language is a learned language which differs depending on the environment of the speaker. While a baby born in Japan and one born in France have the voices and brains to make the same vowel and consonant sounds, they learn to vary the sounds and combine them differently so that their languages sound completely different. In sum, Müller said that the ability to speak phonetic language with intention distinguishes humans from animals.

Language Origin Remains a Mystery

This chapter contains a wide variety of theories, many of them vastly different from one another. They have a common thread only in a general way. They come together because they show human beings at some beginning point inventing a language and a way of thinking, and that beginning marks them as different from animals.

The wide variety of theories presented in this chapter suggests another point. The mystery about the origin of language was far from solved. Philosophers had not been able to agree on any theory—neither divine origin nor invention. By 1895 few thinkers would write or lecture on the topic of language origin because the question seemed unsolvable by the methods used up to that time. Not only was it time for new theories, but it was also time for new methods of study.

After 1900, scientists replaced philosophers, research replaced debate, and evidence replaced speculation. Scholars stopped trying to solve the mystery of language origin as one large concept. With new methods, scholars gathered facts and tried to resolve small questions with answers that could be verified. Scientists from many fields of study gathered evidence that influenced the solution to the language origin mystery. Let us look next at information that significantly altered the old theories and ideas.

This three-year-old girl is teaching her little sister to name familiar objects using the vowel and consonant sounds she learned from her parents.

Four

What Has Science Discovered About Language?

People often like to hang on to their old, comfortable beliefs. The sports fan believes his team is best long after the winning streak has passed. Those who believe life exists only on planet earth scoff at UFO reports. It is not surprising that many people ignored or resisted new scientific findings in the early 1900s when the findings challenged old, common beliefs.

During the late nineteenth and early twentieth centuries, science shook the foundation of the old theories about language origin. Though many people resisted the change brought about by scientific discoveries, many scholars welcomed the information and set a new direction for language origin studies.

Several discoveries affected the way the new scholars studied the mystery. First, geologists had discovered that the earth was much older than anyone had previously thought. Second, Charles Darwin found evidence that all species, including humans, had changed and developed slowly over billions of years. Third, archaeologists found fossils and were able to establish stages in human development. Fourth, a

Opposite is the title page to Charles Lyell's 1868 book.

ELEMENTS

OF

GEOLOGY;

OR,

THE ANCIENT CHANGES OF THE EARTH AND ITS INHABITANTS
AS ILLUSTRATED BY GEOLOGICAL MONUMENTS.

BY SIR CHARLES LYELL, BART., F.R.S.,

AUTHOR OF "PRINCIPLES OF GEOLOGY,"
"GEOLOGICAL EVIDENCES OF THE ANTIQUITY OF MAN," ETC.

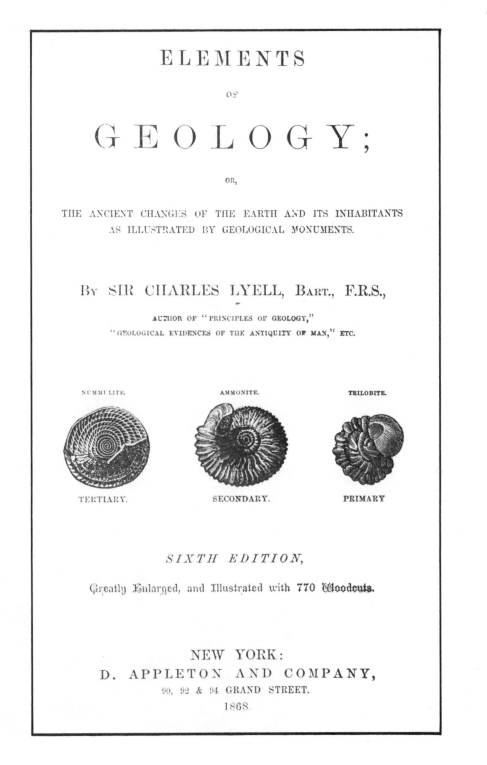

NUMMULITE.   AMMONITE.   TRILOBITE.

TERTIARY.   SECONDARY.   PRIMARY

SIXTH EDITION,

Greatly Enlarged, and Illustrated with **770 Woodcuts.**

NEW YORK:
D. APPLETON AND COMPANY,
90, 92 & 94 GRAND STREET.
1868.

Sir Charles Lyell, considered to be the father of modern geology.

linguist and a doctor studied the human voice mechanism and spelled out how it makes phonetic sounds. Fifth, many scientists did research on the way the brain works, showing how it makes thought and speech possible. These discoveries helped scholars develop new theories about the origin of language.

Why were some of these theories slow to be accepted? How did they affect language scholars' work? Let's look at the age of the earth, the development of the species, the stages of human development, the voice mechanism, and the brain to see what new information affected the old mystery.

The Challenge of the Earth's Age

First, geologists discovered that the earth is billions, not thousands, of years old. When James Hutton, an English geologist, said in the late 1700s that formation of mountains, plains, and oceans "took a long time," few people listened. By the 1830s people did listen to another English geologist, Charles Lyell. He gathered evidence showing that the earth is constantly reshaped by complex geological processes, like volcanoes and earthquakes and erosion. He showed that the earth had been changing for billions of years. His discovery was supported by a French scientist's findings. Boucher de Perthes found tools in the northwest of France that were over three hundred thousand years old.

This illustration from Charles Lyell's *Principles of Geology* shows a volcano formed in the Bay of Naples in 1538. Observations of such formations led to new theories about the age of the earth.

Tools similar to those
Boucher de Perthes
excavated.

The new findings that the earth was billions of years old challenged the old idea that it was six thousand years old. If the earth was so old, people wondered, where had human beings been all that time? Some thought humans were a recent creation on an old earth. Others thought they had lived in the Garden of Eden. Charles Darwin had a different explanation, which provided a second important scientific discovery.

Darwin and Evolution

Charles Darwin, an English biologist, proposed the idea, based on his research, that animal and human life had been evolving slowly over several billion years. Life began on earth, Darwin said, in simple-celled creatures. In order to survive, creatures changed. The strongest lived by developing traits to make them better suited to survive in their environment. Over billions of years creatures became more complex and many varieties developed: sea creatures, land creatures, and air creatures. Several million years ago the primates (apes and monkeys) emerged. Over time, according to Darwin, as their brains and bodies developed further, these primates evolved into the earliest species of humans. Darwin published his theory in 1859 in a book called *Origin of Species*.

Darwin's theory accounted for the age of the earth and the presence of humans, but his idea also challenged the Great Chain of Being idea and the creation story. Darwin's book caused a major uproar because the Great Chain of Being idea said that God had created each species as a link in a long chain of species and had put each species in its place in the

"Instead of evolution through natural selection, some sort of outside intervention was responsible for modern man's most distinctive characteristics."

Jeffrey Goodman,
The Genesis Mystery

"Nor do I believe that any great physical change, as of climate . . . is actually necessary to produce new and unoccupied places for natural selection to fill up."

Charles Darwin, *On the Origin of Species*

This 1861 cartoon is one of many distributed at the time to make fun of Darwin's evolutionary thoughts which were published in his book (below).

ON

THE ORIGIN OF SPECIES

BY MEANS OF NATURAL SELECTION,

OR THE

PRESERVATION OF FAVOURED RACES IN THE STRUGGLE FOR LIFE.

By CHARLES DARWIN, M.A.,

FELLOW OF THE ROYAL, GEOLOGICAL, LINNÆAN, ETC., SOCIETIES;
AUTHOR OF 'JOURNAL OF RESEARCHES DURING H. M. S. BEAGLE'S VOYAGE
ROUND THE WORLD.'

LONDON:
JOHN MURRAY, ALBEMARLE STREET.
1859.

The right of Translation is reserved.

order. They had all been in the same place ever since. Darwin's idea suggested that the species had each developed over time and that humans had evolved from a lower form, from primates, or "monkeys." The public was outraged and drew cartoons of Darwin with an orangutan's body. People were angry that Darwin had opposed the old idea that God had created humans with a pre-set special capacity to receive and invent language. Darwin's theory implied, instead, that human capacity for language had evolved as humans had.

Stages of Human Development

A third discovery further challenged the Great Chain of Being idea and confirmed Darwin's conclusion. Archaeologists dug up ancient fossils and discovered ways to date the old bones. They reconstructed the skeletons and studied skull size, upright position, and use of hands. They used the objects buried among the bones to determine the social order for each species they found.

Their findings, however, came slowly. In 1829 when fossil bones were found in Belgium, few scholars paid attention. By the early 1900s, archaeologists had found fossils in Europe, Africa, Asia, the Middle East, and on the Pacific island of Java and had established stages for the development of humans and their ancestors. According to scientists, human beings developed in four stages over a period of 5.5 million

This stone-age burial was discovered by E. Riviere in 1875. Note the artifacts placed carefully around the skeleton.

An artist's idea of what Australopithecus may have looked like, carrying stick and bone tools.

or more years. For each stage, scientists had found artifacts that suggested how people lived then. What were these stages and when did they occur?

The first stage when a species might be called human occurred between 5.5 million and 1.3 million years ago. The species at this stage is called *Australopithecus*. Members of this species walked on two legs, carried sticks and bone clubs, and lived in groups. They had flat skulls and small brains, capable of communicating in an elaborate system of sounds and gestures, but likely not in many words. David Pilbeam, an anthropologist from Yale University, thought they had very simple speech; anthropologist Raymond Dart thought they did not. Only a few objects or tools have been found with the bones.

Upright Humans

The Australopithecus evolved into the earliest *Homo erectus* (man upright). This second stage began 1.3 million years ago and lasted a million years. Archaeologists have found skeletons of this species on Java Island in the Pacific, China, Africa, and Europe. Three reasons led scientists to conclude that Homo erectus may have developed a language. First, it had a brain 65 percent the size of a modern human brain, a size sufficient for language. Second, the mouth and throat size and development indicate it probably could make the first vowel and consonant sounds. Third,

These three busts have been reconstructed to resemble Pithecanthropus erectus or Homo erectus (left), Neanderthal (center), and Cro-Magnon (right).

its social organization must have required language. According to objects found with the bones, homo erectus planned hunts, divided food-gathering work into separate jobs, formed ties with other bands, and taught skills to the young. These social tasks are complicated, too difficult to accomplish with only grunts and gestures for communication. Scientists think Homo erectus developed a language to carry them out. Anthropologist Grover Kranz thought Homo erectus began to speak about age six, later than modern babies, because Homo erectus had a less-developed brain.

A two million-year-old skull of Australopithecus.

Neanderthal

The third stage of human development, the age of the *Neanderthal*, spanned the time from one hundred thousand to forty thousand years ago. The first skeleton of this species was found in 1856 near Düsseldorf, Germany, in the Neander Valley. Again, archaeologists later found many skeletons throughout the world, an indication that the Neanderthals traveled widely and existed in large numbers. The Neanderthal had a brain the same size as a modern human

Imaginary picture of how Homo erectus may have planned and executed a hunt.

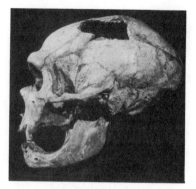

Did Neanderthals look like those in the picture at the right? On the left is a Neanderthal skull found in 1908 by Marcellin Boule used when he tried to reconstruct the skeleton.

brain but had a different-shaped skull. The Neanderthal's throat had a voice mechanism developed low in the throat, the kind capable of making phonetic sounds, the sounds of vowels and consonants. Objects found with Neanderthal fossils suggest that Neanderthals had developed a complex social organization and many tools. One tool was made specifically for a right-handed user, an indication of advanced design ability. All of this combined evidence suggested that the Neanderthals had developed a language.

The fourth human stage began about forty thousand years ago. This species, called the *Cro-Magnon*, looked physically like modern humans with the same brain size, skull shape, and voice mechanism. Remains of this species indicate that they had a highly-developed social and cultural life. Their tools reveal both advanced design and advanced techniques for making them. Their caves display their art. The evidence suggests that the Cro-Magnons had an advanced language, far beyond the original stage.

The Cro-Magnon, with technology, art, and a dignified physical appearance, was a "respectable" ancestor for those who objected to Darwin's idea that humans had evolved from primates, a lower species.

But for years, scientists found no direct ancestor for the Cro-Magnons. For years, scientists thought the Neanderthals had become extinct and had no direct successors. There was a gap, a missing link, between Neanderthals and Cro-Magnons that scientists could not explain.

Recent evidence suggests that Neanderthals *are* the missing link, the ancestors of the Cro-Magnons. For most of the first half of this century, the Neanderthal had a reputation as an ugly, ape-like brute. Today it is considered, at least by some scientists, as "a true human—our ancestor." What caused the change? The story revolves around a scientific error.

In 1908 archaeologists found several Neanderthal skeletons in the south of France. Marcellin Boule,

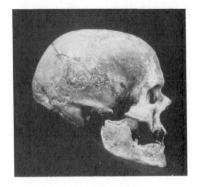

The skull of a Cro-Magnon man.

Possible Cro-Magnon artists at work.

from the French National Museum of Natural History, got the job of reconstructing the bones. When he had them wired together, the Neanderthal man had a curved spine, bent knees, and oddly-shaped feet. He looked like a ''shuffling hunchback.'' Boule said his skull was long and low, signs of mental retardation. He placed him between apes and humans, but much closer to apes. For nearly fifty years, Neanderthals were seen as grunting brutes who mistreated females, looked coarse and shaggy, and slumped along in a bent-knee posture.

Then, in 1957, two physicians, specialists in anatomy, studied Boule's work on the 1908 skeletons. William Strauss of Johns Hopkins University and A.J.E. Cave of St. Bartholomew's Hospital Medical College in London found that Boule had reconstructed the bones wrong. They also found evidence of arthritis, which would have deformed the backbone, making

Scientists pose for a picture at Laugerie Basse, France, in 1908. Neanderthal and Cro-Magnon people lived for hundreds of years in the cliffs of Laugerie Basse.

this skeleton not typical of the species. When they put the bones together correctly, they found the Neanderthal "quite human."

Later Neanderthal skeletons found in the Middle East confirmed Strauss's and Cave's opinion. These skeletons show that Neanderthals had developed nearly as far as the Cro-Magnons. They had well-designed stone tools and a burial ritual. Ralph Solecke of the Smithsonian Institution found Neanderthals in Iraq that had mourned the death of a loved one with flowers. "We should regard him with honor, because almost everything we are directly springs from him," George Constable said in *The Neanderthals*. In spite of evidence, widespread opinion clings to the brutelike image. Old reputations die hard.

Discovery of the age of the earth and the four stages of human development gave students of language origin new and useful information. They could use the information about Australopithecus, Homo erectus, Neanderthal, and Cro-Magnon to discover when, where, and why language began. But they needed additional information to study how the first words began and how they sounded. It took the research of other scientists to discover how the voice mechanism could first make phonetic words.

Voice Mechanism

The voice mechanism in modern speakers works with a system of pipes, valves, and air. Humans have one pathway in the upper throat that divides into two tracks farther down, one for food and one for air. One lower track, the windpipe, has a valve called the *epiglottis*. The epiglottis closes the windpipe so that food cannot get into the lungs and the air in the lungs cannot escape all at once and collapse the lungs. The single pathway above the larynx is a tube with muscles along its walls. It is called the *pharynx*. Its muscles anchor the tongue and move the epiglottis (the valve) open and closed. When the lungs relax after physical

"The Neanderthal is an uncouth and repellent . . . man [whose] nose is not sharply separated from the face, the two being merged in what in another animal would be called a snout."

Eliot Smith, anthropologist

"If he (Neanderthal) could be reincarnated and placed in a New York subway— provided that he were bathed, shaved, and dressed in modern clothing—it is doubtful he would attract any more attention than some of its other denizens [regular riders]."

William Strauss and A.J.E. Cave, anthropologists

Adult vocal tract.

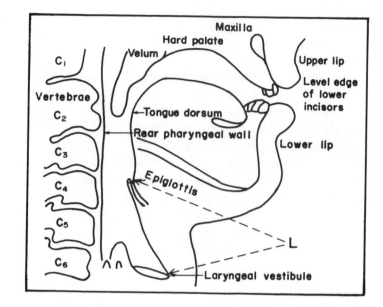

effort, the epiglottis opens and sends air out along the pharynx and out of the mouth. The air rushing out makes the sound of a sigh.

To make vowel and consonant sounds, a person controls the muscles along the pharynx, called *vocal cords*, and controls the placement of the tongue and lips. The rush of air through the larynx, controlled by the vibrations of the vocal cords, is necessary before vowels and consonants can be made. The muscles, or vocal cords, vibrate very quickly as the speaker makes the different sounds of words. Phonetic sounds are possible only if the speaker can send air out through his or her mouth.

Comparing Voice Mechanisms

The voice mechanism in tiny babies (birth to three months) and early primates is different from the adult voice mechanism. Primates originally breathed only through their noses because the larynx was placed high behind the mouth, and there was no pharynx with vocal cords. As primates evolved, the larynx moved down in the throat. Before that move, primates made all sounds by varying the shapes of their mouths. When the larynx had moved part way down into the throat, the voice could make the easiest vowel *a* and a few of the easiest consonants. As the larynx moved lower and as the pharynx became longer, flexibility and vibrations produced the other, more difficult sounds.

Philip Lieberman, a linguist at Brown University, and Dr. Edmund C. Crelin of Yale Medical School studied the voice mechanism of babies and adults, and then reconstructed a clay model of a Homo erectus throat and voice mechanism. They also programmed a computer to measure voice vibrations and volume and tone of each. They discovered that Homo erectus had a voice mechanism similar to a modern child's. They concluded that Homo erectus could form all the vowels and consonants that a modern child can, even though it probably spoke slowly.

The data describing the workings of the voice mechanism and the comparisons among children, adults, and Homo erectus offered language origin scholars a better chance to tell when language began.

How Does the Brain Make Words?

Although the development of the voice mechanism is necessary for phonetic words, the development of the brain is necessary to give phonetic words their meaning. Scientists who identified the parts of the brain and how they work together to give words meaning provided additional data useful to language origin scholars.

Many scientists contributed to the explanation of the brain's mental process. Five areas work together very quickly to make words that have meaning. They enable the brain to take in information from the five senses, sort it, give it meaning, and then instruct the voice mechanism to work. Each of the five areas has a different function.

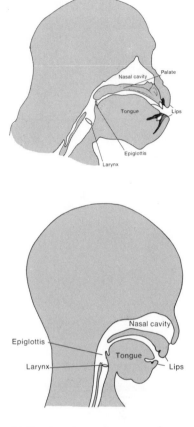

At the top is a diagram of the head and neck of a young adult chimpanzee which shows the vocal tract. The lower diagram shows the vocal system of a human fetus at seven months.

This map of a human brain charts all the areas associated with the formation of speech.

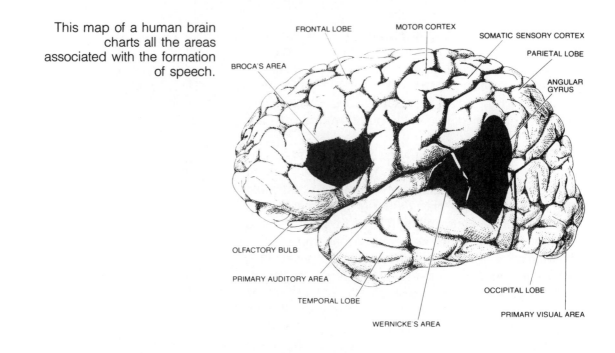

FRONTAL LOBE MOTOR CORTEX SOMATIC SENSORY CORTEX PARIETAL LOBE ANGULAR GYRUS BROCA'S AREA OLFACTORY BULB PRIMARY AUDITORY AREA TEMPORAL LOBE WERNICKE'S AREA OCCIPITAL LOBE PRIMARY VISUAL AREA

First, there is the *cerebral cortex*, a thin layer of nerve cells covering the outer surface of both halves of the brain. The cerebral cortex has different areas to receive information from the outside world through the five senses. For example, one area registers the sight of a white lamb, another registers the sound of its bleating.

Second, there is the *angular gyrus* near the cerebral cortex. The angular gyrus operates as a connecting station, associating a signal from one sense with a signal from another. For example, it would connect the sight of the white lamb with the bleating sound with the softness of its wool when the hand touches it. The angular gyrus allows people to learn vocabulary words because it connects the sight of a lamb with the sound of the word *lamb*. The function of the angular gyrus verified Locke's and Herder's theories described as reflection.

Third, there is the *Wernicke's area* located in a

middle portion of the brain. This area works as a selector and retriever, picking appropriate vocabulary out of the storehouse of words to go with the information from the senses. This area gives meaning to word sounds.

Fourth, there is the *Broca's area* near the front of the brain. Its function is to give messages to the area of the brain that controls the face muscles, the jaw, the tongue, the palate, and the larynx. The Broca's area works with the Wernicke's area and serves as a transfer station. For example, the Wernicke's area selects *lamb* out of all its words on record, and the Broca's area transforms the *lamb* selection into messages to the body parts that make the sound *lamb*.

Fifth, there is the *arcuate fasciculus*, a bundle of nerve fibers. They transfer messages from one part of the brain to another.

These five parts, developed and working together, are necessary before the brain can make words with meanings. Homo erectus had a brain 65 percent the size of an adult human brain. Homo erectus' brain was large enough to have all five necessary parts, enough to make words and sentences with at least simple meanings.

The Limbic System

An explanation of one other part in the brain system helps to distinguish animal sounds from human words. Both humans and animals have a *limbic system* located at the core, or center, of the brain. It has two functions. First, it receives messages from the external world through the senses and stirs the body to feel and to react physically to hunger, fear, rage, and excitement. For example, the sound of someone following in a dark alley would send a message to the limbic system and cause the body to shake and the heart to pound. Its second function is to make the body react instinctively. The limbic system sets the body running or screaming as an automatic response instead of a thought-out decision.

"One of the great 'mysteries' is the sudden acceleration in the rate of change of human culture that occurred between 40,000 and 30,000 years ago."

Philip Lieberman, *On the Origins of Language*

"The development of a modern pharynx, with its huge potential for communication could very well explain a quantum leap in physical and cultural evolution."

George Constable, *The Neanderthals*

Experiments to teach chimpanzees to talk in words have largely failed, even though they have brains similar to human brains, though less developed. In monkeys and apes the angular gyrus is too small to sort information from the outside world and send it to the Wernicke's area for meaning. Instead, information from the senses goes directly to the limbic system when the sorting breaks down at the connecting station, the angular gyrus. The information stimulates feeling in the limbic system and produces an automatic response. Earlier theorists, discussed in chapter 3, pointed out the difference between animal sounds made by instinct and human, phonetic sounds made intentionally. The discovery of how the brain works explains that difference. Sounds made by instinct probably originate in the limbic system; phonetic sounds made intentionally result from the five brain parts working together.

Trying to teach a chimp to speak is no easy task.

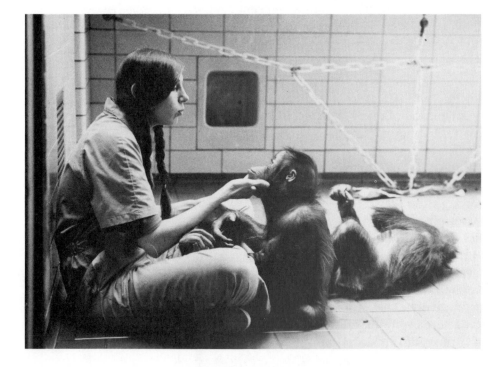

In summary, the age of the earth and the long, slow evolution of its species, the stages of prehistoric humans, the workings of the voice and brain—these were the discoveries that challenged old theories and sometimes shocked those who believed the biblical creation story was literally true. These are the research results that gave scholars interested in the origin of language new information to use in developing new theories. How did they draw the facts together and build on them? Let us look at three modern language origin theories to find out about new solutions to the old mystery.

Five

What Do People Today Believe About Language Origin?

Trying to solve the mystery of language origin in the early days was like putting together a child's first wooden puzzle. Scholars worked with a few big pieces and fit them together into simple pictures. After scientific data of many kinds became available to language scholars, the puzzle became harder. Solving the mystery then was like putting together a one thousand-piece puzzle of a picture mostly composed of water and trees, the kind where eighty pieces look alike and seem to fit nowhere and everywhere. Developing a simple solution may have been easier, but it did not offer the best answer. Curious researchers are never satisfied until they find the best possible answer, even when they are faced with an extremely complex task.

Philip Lieberman, the author of *The Biology and Evolution of Language*, believes that language origin must be studied in connection with psychology, sociology, physiology, paleontology, anthropology, archaeology, and linguistic science. In his 1975 book, *On the Origin of Language*, he states that because language is part of everything humans do, "Everything depends on everything else." Obviously nobody

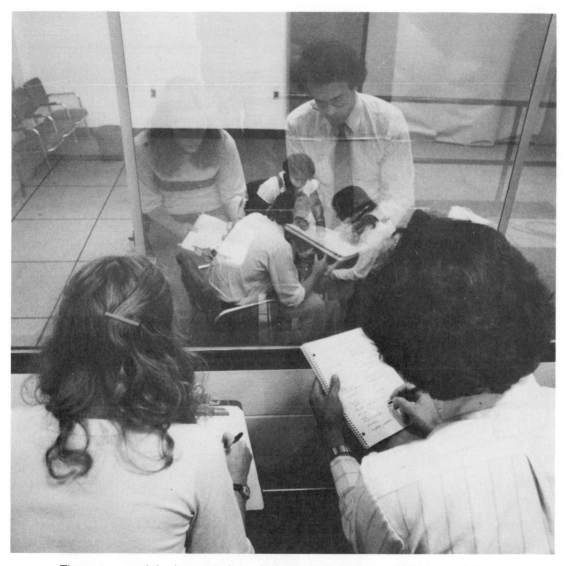

These two sociologists are observing an adult and two adolescents interact.
The scientists are researching human development and learning patterns.
The data they collect will add to the fund of knowledge used to
formulate scientific theories.

Philip Lieberman is a linguist at Brown University, working in the department of cognitive and linguistic sciences.

knows everything about everything. But as scholars saw language in ever more complex ways, their theories too became more complex and attempted to answer more of the who, what, why, when, where, and how questions in a single theory.

Many scholars did their homework, studying and combining data from many different fields. They studied the stages of human evolution, speech development in children, experiments with primates, the psychology of learning, linguists' findings from old texts, and comparative languages. They developed origin theories based on verifiable evidence. They had much evidence, but the question remains whether they know enough yet to say accurately how language began. Among the important twentieth-century language

This group of apes, reminiscent of Australopithecus, lives comfortably in the trees but also has begun to be comfortable on the ground.

origin scholars are Grace de Laguna, Geza Révész, and A.S. Diamond.

Grace de Laguna, an American psychologist whose work was published in 1963, said the need for social control caused primitive people to develop language in the first place. She began her theory at a stage before Australopithecus.

Early in evolution, Laguna said, primates were tree dwellers with bodies adapted for climbing and swinging. Eventually, a species of primates moved to the ground and their bodies and their social order changed. They began to walk upright, their arms grew shorter, and they began to look more like modern humans. Because ground living had more dangers than tree living, they needed a new system of social control to protect the members of the group. Out of the developing social control, language originated, Laguna said.

A Japanese macaque sits on guard, ready to give a screech for danger, if necessary, to the rest of the group.

Baboons communicate the danger of a tiger in the grass while baring their teeth in a threat.

While still at the animal stage, one primate instinctively warned others when it detected danger. If one monkey screeched, the others took cover. Many evolutionary ages later, the brain had developed and one pre-human could communicate a specific kind of danger and designate whether to run or hide or fight. Yet farther along in evolution, one member could warn of danger and another member could respond. The ability to give verbal response marked the beginning of language, Laguna said. At that point two members communicated with each other.

Over those millions of years, the evolution of the brain made greater communication possible. Laguna thought that the process occurred by *specification* and *designation*. *Specification* means being able to notice increasingly more specific situations. *Designation* means being able to give commands for increasingly complex and precise plans of action. At first a member of the group could specify general danger only when it was close enough to see. Later, the member could use clues in the environment to figure out a specific enemy while it was still at a distance and, as a result, give other members a complex plan to act before the enemy arrived.

The practice of specifying danger and designating the best reaction developed the brain and made it capable of greater complexity. By repeating the process, the brain developed a larger memory, and the instincts became more refined. Eventually, the brain created words.

Developing Conversation

According to Laguna, nouns, or naming words, appeared first, in order to name or identify the danger. Verbs, or command words, appeared next, in order to direct the members to safety. Finally, speakers developed conversation, which Laguna identified as questions and answers.

The development may have gone something like this: A prehistoric woman might have noticed danger and said, "hippo," a noun. It really meant, "We are in danger of attack by a hippopotamus." Later, she might have said, "run," a verb which really meant, "Run into the bushes to hide from the hippopotamus." Later, after her brain had evolved, she could designate more accurately. "Run bushes fast," she might have commanded. At the naming and command levels, the speaker expected only to be heard. At the question stage, the speaker expected to be heard and also expected an answer. "Hippo?" one might say as he came out of the bushes. The guard might have responded, "Hippo go river." By Laguna's definition, language began when a conversation occurred between two people.

In sum, Laguna's social control theory began with primates that maintained control of their groups with instinctive cries. The next step, specified warnings and

"Were the first words, therefore, verbs? Are not verbs the words of significant action? And do not verbs by themselves make sense, as when we cry, *Stop! Run! Out!* Words of command might also have served early man."

James L. Ludovici,
Origins of Language

"The first words must have been as concrete and specialized in meaning as possible. Now, what are the words whose meaning is the most concrete and the most specialized? Without any doubt proper names."

Otto Jespersen, *Language: Its Nature, Development and Origin*

Lobo hurriedly points out
a poisonous snake.

designated commands, developed with Australopithecus. Homo erectus was capable of using nouns and
verbs, questions and answers. This language development spanned at least five million years.

Language as Social Contact

Geza Révész, a twentieth-century Dutch psychologist, whose work was published in 1956, also developed a theory of language origin that integrated several
different kinds of evidence. He too explained the cause
or purpose for language, the stages in its development,
the process by which the brain evolved, and the kind
of words spoken at the beginning. But Révész inter-
preted the evidence differently than Laguna did.

Révész said language developed for the purpose
of social *contact*, not social control. Both animals and
humans, he said, have always needed contact with
others of their kind.

Révész, like Laguna, began his theory at the animal level and explained the developments that led to language. Like Laguna, Révész also described language development in three stages, but they are different stages. Contact with others began at the *instinct stage*, developed to the *emotional stage*, and developed further to the *intellect stage*.

At the simplest, instinct stage, animals herded to graze, and they formed packs for protection. Their simple play involved running together and chasing, bumping, and nudging others in simple physical contact. Birds instinctively made nests together and sang instinctively to mate. Sounds animals made at this level Révész called *cries*.

The second stage involves feelings and emotions that both animals and humans experience, both in prehistory and today. For example, monkeys and people jump and scream together in excitement. When a person pets a cat, it purrs with pleasure. People *ohh* and *ahh* over northern lights and Fourth-of-July fireworks. These examples represent feelings and emotions shared in contact with others, the kind of experiences that go back to the earliest stages of human

The wapiti graze together for protection and for social contact (left). Birds rely on instinct when nesting and mating (right).

On the left, the Minnesota Twins exhibit their joy at winning the 1987 World Series. On the right, a cat enjoys the rubbing and scratching it is receiving.

contact. Révész identified communication of these kinds of feelings and emotions as *calls*.

The third stage involved the intellect—thinking—and used words. This stage applied to humans but not animals. Human beings spoke words, Révész said, when the brain was able to make a symbol. A vocal sound is a symbol when it brings to the speaker's mind an absent object or a past experience. For example, when a speaker says *fire* and his mind thinks of fire but none is present, the word acts as a symbol. Language began when the brain could make a symbol, Révész said.

According to Révész, the brain evolved over millions of years and, consequently, people's expressions evolved from instinctive cries to emotional calls to intellectual symbols. Révész called the process which helped the brain evolve *generalization*. Generalizing works according to the pattern Locke called "association of ideas" and Herder called "reflection." Révész said the brain first sees objects separately. Second, it notices how objects are similar and different. Third, the brain formulates an idea about the similar objects. The brain began with simple generalizations and evolved into more complex ones.

For example, a prehistoric person might have sampled two roots and found them both to taste good. He generalized that he could eat that kind of root. Later, he noticed that he also ate berries and meat, and he generalized *food*, a more complex idea. Or he snapped one stick and then another and realized he *broke* sticks. Later, he saw the similarity between *breaking* a stick and *breaking* an animal into parts to eat. The sound for *break* at that point became a symbol for the action. Repeating the process—seeing, connecting, forming ideas—developed the thinking brain, the intellect.

Language as Sentences

The Révész theory says that language developed in sentences, not sounds or words. The sentences, as others have described, were short, at first only one word. Unlike Laguna who thought nouns were the first words, Révész thought language began with command sentences. Command "sentences" were really verbs calling for action: "come," "break," "run," "hit." The second kind of sentence that evolved was a statement, or information sentence: "dog barks," "fire hot," "foot hurts." Finally, like Laguna, Révész thought speakers asked questions and sought answers. These were the beginnings of conversation. "Berry patch?" one member of the group might have asked of another. "In woods," another might have responded. Révész thought that early speakers designated all three stages—commands, statements, and questions—by means of voice sounds, by varying the pitch and tone of the voice. For example, the voice goes up at the end of a sentence when a speaker asks a question.

Both Laguna and Révész went back to the animal stage to find the language source. Both Laguna and Révész focused attention on causes, but they disagreed on the kind of causes; Laguna said language developed for social control and Révész said it was for social

"It would be more nearly true to say that language began with sentences than words."

Grace de Laguna, *Speech: Its Function and Development*

"Speech appeared first as one indistinct nondescript vowel and a small number of comparatively precise consonants."

A.S. Diamond, *The History and Origin of Language*

This grimacing basketball player only needs a short informative sentence to let his teammates know what the problem is.

contact. Both said language developed in three stages ending with questions and answers. Laguna said nouns came first and verbs second; Révész said verbs came first and information sentences second. Laguna said thought developed by specification and differentiation; Révész said it developed by generalization. Both Laguna's "warning" and Révész's "cry" go back to animal stages. Révész's "call" stage fits what we know of Australopithecus. The intellect, symbol, and complex generalizations began with homo erectus but did not develop until the Neanderthal. From animal to Neanderthal spanned more than 5.5 million years.

Language Develops Through Trial and Error

A third twentieth-century theory about language origin also grew out of scientific evidence; Dr. A.S. Diamond, an American sociologist whose work was

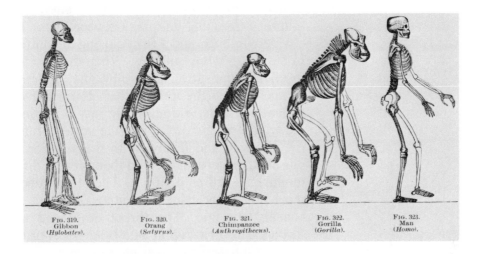

FIG. 320.
Orang
(Satyrus).

FIG. 321.
Chimpanzee
(Anthropithecus).

FIG. 322.
Gorilla
(Gorilla).

FIG. 323.
Man
(Homo).

published in 1959, also tried to solve the mystery in this way. Diamond's theory pays minimal attention to source, causes, and thought development. His theory focuses on the first sounds and words. While Diamond based parts of his theory on the research findings of others, he did extensive research himself into old texts and comparative languages.

Diamond said that the physical changes leading to language happened by accident. He explained that the larynx originally developed, not for speech, but to make it possible to use lungs and to breathe air. The larynx was originally connected to the arm muscles and worked like a string that pulls a bag closed. During strenuous and active arm movements, the larynx pulled the top of the windpipe closed. When it was closed, the mouth was also closed, no air was exhaled, and no sound was possible. When the strenuous arm movement stopped, the muscles relaxed the larynx to let air out of the lungs and allow breathing to resume.

Diamond explained that the physical structure of the throat changed when a primate species moved from tree dwelling to land dwelling. While in trees, these

Taken from Haeckel's *Evolution of Man*, this chart represents millions of years of evolution.

primates often used their arms strenuously for climbing trees and jumping between them. They had a wide windpipe and a firm closing to control the air in the lungs while moving. When they became land dwellers, the strenuous climbing and swinging stopped. Then the muscle that closed the windpipe softened and deteriorated, the larynx moved lower, the windpipe narrowed, and the vocal cords became round-edged and fleshy. With the separation of the muscles, this creature could then breathe through his mouth, as well as his nose. The larynx became the mechanism that made the sounds of vowels and consonants possible. The throat developed a speech mechanism by accident as a by-product of a change in the primates' physical environment.

Diamond's theory indicates that the ability to think also evolved accidentally. He said that rather than going through a series of stages, thought appeared in a continuous line of increased perception. The whole development occurred by trial and error. A puppy, for

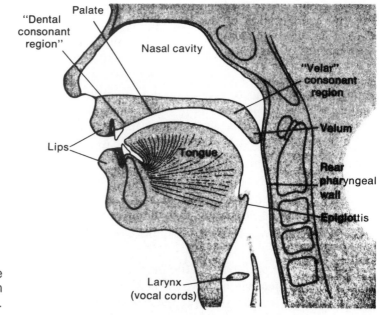

Note the position of the larynx in this modern adult vocal tract.

example, can learn how to get out of a fenced-in area if it tries enough ways and accidentally finds the hole big enough. Once the hole is found, the puppy can remember to use it again. Primates and the earliest humans used the same trial-and-error method and gradually saw how to improve their hunting skills, their tools, and their communication, one small step at a time.

Diamond believes that at first animals had only instinct, an unlearned feeling or striving "leading to action." Gradually, primates developed cognition, or awareness. They were aware that they could deliberately do some action—do it on purpose. They could use their arms in large gestures and make loud sounds. They could swing sticks and shout harshly during a hunt. In a continuous process of trial and error, they refined their language of gestures and cries. When the voice mechanism had evolved, the sounds became phonetic and the gestures fewer. In short, language developed by accident, or at least without intent, when the voice could make the sounds and the trial-and-error method had taught the speakers enough recognition.

"Without some capacity for disinterested social play . . . our ancestors would probably never have developed human speech."

Grace de Laguna, *Speech: Its Function and Development*

"To express a desire, to intimate and order, to denote a taking possession of persons or of things—these were the first uses of language."

A.S. Diamond, *The History and Origin of Language*

For those whose hearing mechanisms do not function, a system of gestures is still one of the most-used methods of communication. An interpreter uses sign language here to translate the speaker's words.

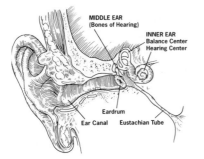

Diagram of the human ear showing the hearing mechanism.

Diamond also pointed out that the ear had to be developed enough to hear phonetic sounds before there was language. Speech sounds are heard by a series of rhythmical pressures of air on the eardrum. These rhythmical disturbances of air are very gentle and very rapid. Until the eardrum had evolved a sensitivity to phonetic sounds, no listener could distinguish the words of a speaker.

To develop his ideas about how words evolved, Diamond studied ancient written texts and also compared today's languages. From this collective evidence, he developed a theory about the first sounds, the first words, and the first sentences.

Speech Sounds

According to Diamond, the first speech sounds were consonants and the *a* vowel, the sounds easiest to make. Vowels are harder to form than consonants, except for the *a* which can be made without moving the tongue or mouth. Generally, there are three categories of consonants: *nasals*, *n*, *m*, and *ng*, which are made in the nasal passage; *plosives*, *p*, *b*, *t*, *d*, *k*, *g*, which are made with a burst of air out of the mouth; and *fricatives*, *f*, *v*, *th*, *s*, *z*, *sh*, *zh*, which require more control in the throat. There are a few additional consonants, the *l*, *r*, *j*, and *w*, which are made low in the throat.

Diamond said that the nasals and plosives were the first phonetic sounds the voice could make, plus the *a* vowel. The other vowels, *e*, *i*, *o*, *u*, and the fricative consonants could be made only when the larynx had moved farther down in the throat. The vocal cords then had a long enough space for the greater vibrations needed for those sounds. At first, Diamond said, the voice was slow to blend sounds. It could make *c*, *a*, *p*, separately and blend them into *cap* slowly.

Since the voice worked slowly, Diamond thought the first words were short. He thought there were three

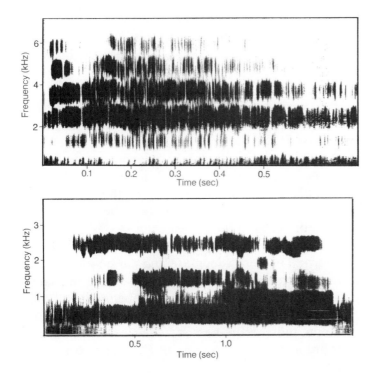

At the top is a spectrogram (a picture made by a spectrograph machine to record a series of sound waves) of a loud chimpanzee cry that sounded like "aw." The bottom spectrogram shows how a similar cry of "schwa" from a three-year-old gorilla looks.

patterns: *c v* (consonant, vowel) as in *da*; *c v c*, as in *bap*; and *c v c v*, as in *nana*. Diamond thought the first words were verbs, action words. Nouns (naming words) developed from verbs, and adjectives (descriptive words) developed from nouns and verbs. Diamond said that all the early short words were requests for help. They all meant some form of violent action: "hit," "smash," "crush," "kill," "cut." Those were the actions, Diamond said, that early people needed help with.

Diamond next concluded, as Révész did, that sentences developed in an order. But the two scholars envisioned different kinds of order. Both said that commands came first in one-word sentences. "Hit," an early speaker might have told a helper. Both said that information or fact sentences came second. "John crushes," one speaker might have informed another.

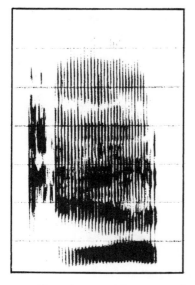

Here is a spectrogram of the word "cat" spoken by a person into a microphone.

Révész said that questions and answers came third, but Diamond thought descriptive sentences came third. "Ilsa is careful," a speaker might have described.

Diamond's theory about the development of sounds, words, and sentences was developed from patterns observed in later language and assumed to be true as well for the first language. From extensive study of written texts and today's languages, he found patterns. The earliest known root words describe violent action. Diamond's studies on the percentages of verbs, nouns, and adjectives show the highest percentage of verbs in the oldest texts. As he read texts from more and more recent time periods, he found a pattern: The verbs decrease and the nouns and adjectives increase. Diamond concluded that the same pattern would have been true at the beginning of language. In today's languages nasal sounds are the most common, plosives are next in frequency, and the fricatives are least common. Again, Diamond concluded that the same pattern occurred at the beginning of language.

Diamond's theory about nasal and plosive sounds and verbs seems to fit what we know of Homo erectus. The more difficult consonants and vowels and the fact and descriptive sentences seem to fit Neanderthal. The gestures and loud sounds that preceded

"The north wind and the sun" was the phrase spoken and recorded here.

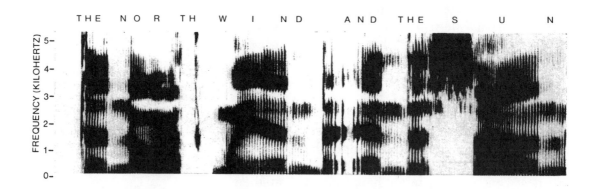

The Forms of Communication and Their Position in Evolution and Linguistic History

		FORMS OF CONTACT				
		FORMS OF COMMUNICATION				
		Non-linguistic (non-verbal)		Linguistic		
		(i)	(ii)	(iii)	(iv)	(v)
Stage	Need for making contact	Intended indication of vital needs	Demands addressed to individuals	Imperative language	Language with primitive structure	Fully developed language
Medium	Contact sound	Cry	Call	Word		
Rank in Evolution	Antecedent of communication	Archaic form of communication	Primitive form of communication	Archaic form of language	Primitive form of language	Fully developed language
		Prehistory		Proto-history		Linguistic history

Occurrence:
In animals..→
In man ....→

phonetic language seem to go back to Australopithecus. The total span covered over five million years.

What Has Been Solved? What Remains?

A review of three twentieth-century theories shows that some things in the mystery of language origin are partially settled. It seems safe to say that language developed slowly over millions of years, that the first language was slow and limited, and that language developed out of some human need. But those conclusions are very general. The specific questions and answers remain a mystery. We can guess what early speakers might have said, but what did they actually say? When did they say it? Why did they speak? And who were they?

A table from Révész's book *The Origins and Prehistory of Language* shows how language developed from a contact sound, to a cry, to a call, to a word.

Conclusion

The Search Goes On

Language with its many millions of speakers and its many thousands of varieties fascinates lay people as well as scholars. As we search on, we discover more and more small questions that may help to answer the big question.

Archaeologists may find more bones, and thus learn more about the appearance and development of our ancestors. But the brain and the voice that made the first words were gone millions of years ago. The solution to the mystery of language origin will come, if it ever does, from the small studies done by many different people. These bits and pieces may someday click together to solve the great puzzle of where, when, and how human language began.

As long as the mystery remains, we will continue to search for answers because language, as Diamond said, ''records the mental and material history of man.'' We want to know how it began; it is our nature to search.

Poet Robert Herrick wrote,

> Attempt the end, and never stand to doubt,
> Nothing's so hard but search will find it out.

Perhaps over time his advice and optimism will be proved true about the mystery of language origin.

Glossary

analogy a comparison that suggests that if two things agree with one another in some respects they will probably agree in others

anatomy a science specializing in body structure, its parts, and their function

anthropoid an early being resembling a human in shape, an ape in action

anthropologist a person who studies humans in relation to origin, race, physical characteristics, environment, social relations, and culture

archaeologist a person who studies fossils, artifacts, and monuments of past human life and activities

arthritis a disease that causes inflammation of the joints

articulate able to speak clearly and effectively

associate to bring together in any of various ways, as in memory or imagination

confirm to strengthen, to prove

controversy an argument, a discussion marked by opposing viewpoints

denizens people or animals who frequently go to a particular place

derive to take from a source

divine relating to a god

eardrum a thin layer of skin separating the middle ear from the external ear

endowed enriched, provided with natural capacity, power, or ability

extinct no longer existing

fricatives speech sounds made by vibrations deep in the throat (f, v, th, s, z, sh, zh)

generalization to conclude a general idea from facts, statistics, or specific information

geologist a person who studies the history of the earth especially as recorded in rocks

gestures movements made by body or limbs as a means of expression

hypothesis an explanation used to account for certain facts and as a basis for further investigation

inanimate lacking consciousness, not endowed with life, such as a rock or chair

inhabitants residents of a place

instinct a response not based on thought or reason, behavior that occurs naturally, below the conscious level

intellect the power of the mind, the capacity for thinking and acquiring knowledge

linguist   a person who studies language
logic   a particular method of reasoning and thinking

minimal   least possible, small
myth   story that illustrates the world view of a people and reveals their beliefs

nasals   speech sounds issuing through the nose (m, n, ng)
nerve fibers   many strands of connecting nerve tissues

opponents   those on opposite sides of a debate

paleontologist   one who studies life in former geologic periods by examining fossil animals and
   plants
philologist   a person who studies human speech, especially the study of literature
philosopher   a person who uses logical reasoning to search for an understanding of the basic
   truths and principles of the universe, life, morals, and human perception
plosives   speech sounds made by the forced release of air through the mouth (b, p, d, t, g, k)
primates   the family that includes apes, monkeys, and humans
primordial   the earliest formed or developed
psychologist   a person who studies the science of the mind and human behavior

reside   to be present

sequence   ordered in time, first one and then another
sociologist   one who studies the science of origin, development, organization, and functioning of
   human society
span   a distance or space extended between two points
specification   the act of giving a detailed description
speech pathologist   a person who studies abnormalities in speech
spontaneous   arising from momentary impulses, without plan or effort

theologian   a person who specializes in the interpretation of religious faith, practice, and
   experience

unconsciously   not deliberately planned or carried out

verifiable   able to prove the truth of, able to be confirmed

For Further Exploration

Jean Aitchison, *Linguistics*. New York: David McKay & Co., Inc., 1978.

Charles Berlitz, *Native Tongues*. New York: Grosset & Dunlap Publishers, 1982.

Robert Clairborne, *Our Marvelous Native Tongue: The Life and Times of the English Language*. New York: Times Books, 1983.

Robert Clairborne, et al., eds., *Word Mysteries and Histories*. Boston: Houghton Mifflin Company, 1986.

Virginia P. Clark, et al., *Language: Introductory Readings*. New York: St. Martin's Press, 1981.

Robert Finn, "Origin of Speech," *Science Digest*, August 1982, 52+.

Roger Lewin, "Anthropologist Argues That Language Cannot Be Read in Stones," *Science*, July 4, 1986, 23+.

Philip Lieberman, *The Biology and Evolution of Language*. Cambridge: Harvard University Press, 1984.

Robert McCrum, et al., *The Story of English*. New York: Viking Press, 1986.

Mario Pei, *The Story of Language*. New York: J.B. Lippincott Company, 1965.

David S. Thompson, *Language*. New York: Time-Life Books, 1975.

Stephen Ullmann, *Semantics: An Introduction to the Science of Meaning*. New York: Barnes and Noble, 1979.

William S-Y. Wang, intro., *Human Communication: Language and Its Psychobiological Bases*. San Francisco: W.H. Freeman and Company, 1982.

Additional Bibliography

George Constable and eds., *The Neanderthals*. New York: Time-Life Books, 1973.

Grace Andrus de Laguna, *Speech: Its Function and Development*. Bloomington: Indiana University Press, 1963.

A.S. Diamond, LL.D., *The History and Origin of Language*. New York: Philosophical Society, 1959.

Maitland Edey and eds., *The Missing Link*. New York: Time-Life Books, 1972.

Northrop Frye, *The Educated Imagination*. Toronto: The Hunter Rose Company, 1963.

Paul A. Gaeng, *Introductions to the Principles of Language*. Lanham, MD: University Press of America, 1971.

F. Clark Howell and eds., *Early Man*. New York: Time-Life Books, 1965.

Helene Laird and Charlton, *The Tree of Language*. Cleveland: The World Publishing Company, 1959.

Philip Lieberman, *On the Origins of Language*. New York: Macmillan Publishing Co., Inc., 1975.

L.J. Ludovici, *Origins of Language*. New York: G.P. Putnam's Sons, 1965.

Mario Pei, *The Story of Language*. New York: J.B. Lippincott Company, 1965.

Tom Prideaux and eds., *Cro-Magnon Man*. New York: Time-Life Books, 1973.

G. Révész, *The Origins and Prehistory of Language*. New York: Philosophical Library, 1956.

James H. Stam, *Inquiries into the Origin of Language: The Fate of a Question*. New York: Harper and Row, Publishers, 1976.

Leopold Stein, *The Infancy of Speech and the Speech of Infancy*. London: Mitheren and Co., Ltd., 1949.

Edmund White, et al. and eds., *The First Men*. New York: Time-Life Books, 1973.

Index

About the Author

Clarice Swisher lives in St. Paul, Minnesota. Throughout her career as an educator, she has both studied and taught literature and language: American and British literature, history of the English language, and reading. Aside from her career, she enjoys London, theoretical physics, her dog Annie, and her red sports car.

Picture Credits